TRUE STORIES OF GREAT AMERICANS

THEODORE ROOSEVELT

MR. ROOSEVELT AT SAGAMORE HILL

THEODORE ROOSEVELT

BY

EDMUND LESTER PEARSON

20-16084

New York

THE MACMILLAN COMPANY

1920

ACKNOWLEDGMENT

The author wishes to express his gratitude for permission to refer to the works which have been consulted in writing this book.
book.

First and foremost, to Mr. William Roscoe Thayer, for " Theodore Roosevelt; An Intimate Biography." (Houghton, Mifflin Co.)

To Messrs. Charles Scribner's Sons for these writings of Theodore Roosevelt: " African Game Trails "; " Theodore Roosevelt: An Autobiography "; " The Rough Riders "; " Through the Brazilian Wilderness "; " History as Literature." And for " Theodore Roosevelt and His Time " by Joseph Bucklin Bishop, in *Scribner's Magazine,* for December, 1919.

To Messrs. Harper and Brothers and to Mr. Hermann Hagedorn for " The Boys' Life of Theodore Roosevelt " by Hermann Hagedorn.

To The Century Company for these books by Theodore Roosevelt: " The Strenuous Life "; " Ranch Life and the Hunting Trail."

To Messrs. G. P. Putnam's Sons for these books by Theodore Roosevelt: " American Ideals "; " The Wilderness Hunter."

ACKNOWLEDGMENT

To Mr. Charles G. Washburn for his " Theodore Roosevelt; the Logic of His Career." (Houghton, Mifflin Co.)

To Messrs Doubleday, Page & Co. and to Mr. Lawrence F. Abbott for " Impressions of Theodore Roosevelt " by Lawrence F. Abbott.

CONTENTS

LIST OF ILLUSTRATIONS

THEODORE ROOSEVELT

CHAPTER I

THE BOY WHO COLLECTED ANIMALS

IF you had been in New York in 1917 or 1918
you might have seen, walking quickly from a
shop or a hotel to an automobile, a thick-set but active and muscular man, wearing a soft black hat
and a cape overcoat. Probably there would have
been a group of people waiting on the sidewalk,
as he came out, for this was Theodore Roosevelt, Ex-President of the United States, and there
were more Americans who cared to know what
he was doing, and to hear what he was saying,
than cared about any other living man.

Although he was then a private citizen, holding
no office, he was a leader of his country, which
was engaged in the Great War. Americans were
being called upon,— the younger men to risk
their lives in battle, and the older people to suffer
and support their losses. Theodore Roosevelt
had always said that it was a good citizen's duty

cheerfully to do one or the other of these things in
the hour of danger.　They knew that he had done
both; and so it was to him that men turned, as
to a strong and brave man, whose words were
simple and noble, and what was more important,
whose actions squared with his words.

He had come back, not long before, from one
of his hunting trips, and it was said that fever
was still troubling him.　The people wish to
know if this is true, and one of the men on the
sidewalk, a reporter, probably, steps forward and
asks him a question.

He stops for a moment, and turns toward the
man.　Not much thought of sickness is left in
the mind of any one there!　His face is clear,
his cheeks ruddy,— the face of a man who lives
outdoors; and his eyes, light-blue in color, look
straight at the questioner.　One of his eyes, it
had been said, was dimmed or blinded by a blow
while boxing, years before, when he was President.　But no one can see anything the matter
with the eyes; they twinkle in a smile, and as his
face puckers up, and his white teeth show for an
instant under his light-brown moustache, the
group of people all smile, too.

His face is so familiar to them,— it is as if they
were looking at somebody they knew as well as
their own brothers.　The newspaper cartoonists

had shown it to them for years. No one else smiled like that; no one else spoke so vigorously.

"Never felt better in my life!" he answers, bending toward the man.

"But thank you for asking!" and there is a pleasant and friendly note in his voice, which perhaps surprises some of those who, though they had heard much of his emphatic speech, knew but little of his gentleness. He waves his hand, steps into the automobile, and is gone.

Theodore Roosevelt was born October 27, 1858, in New York City, at 28 East Twentieth Street. The first Roosevelt of his family to come to this country was Klaes Martensen van Roosevelt who came from Holland to what is now New York about 1644. He was a "settler," and that, says Theodore Roosevelt, remembering the silly claims many people like to make about their long-dead ancestors, is a fine name for an immigrant, who came over in the steerage of a sailing ship in the seventeenth century instead of the steerage of a steamer in the nineteenth century. From that time, for the next seven generations, from father to son, every one of the family was born on Manhattan Island. As New Yorkers say, they were "straight New York."

Immigrant or settler, or whatever Klaes van

Roosevelt may have been, his children and grand-children had in them more than ordinary ability. They were not content to stand still, but made themselves useful and prosperous, so that the name was known and honored in the city and State even before the birth of the son who was to make it illustrious throughout the world.

"My father," says the President, "was the best man I ever knew. . . . He never physically punished me but once, but he was the only man of whom I was ever really afraid." The elder Roosevelt was a merchant, a man courageous and gentle, fond of horses and country life. He worked hard at his business, for the Sanitary Commission during the Civil War, and for the poor and unfortunate of his own city, so hard that he wore himself out and died at forty-six. The President's mother was Martha Bulloch from Georgia. Two of her brothers were in the Confederate Navy, so while the Civil War was going on, and Theodore Roosevelt was a little boy, his family like so many other American families, had in it those who wished well for the South, and those who hoped for the success of the North.

Many American Presidents have been poor when they were boys. They have had to work hard, to make a way for themselves, and the same strength and courage with which they did this has later helped to bring them into the White House. It has seemed as if there were magic connected with being born in a log-cabin, or having to work hard to get an education, so that only the boys who did this could become famous.   Of course it is what is in the boy himself, together with the effect his life has had on him, that counts.   The boy whose family is rich, or even well-off, has something to struggle against, too.   For with these it is easy to slip into comfortable and lazy ways, to do nothing because one does not have to do anything.   Some men never rise because their early life was too hard; some, because it was too easy.

Roosevelt might have had the latter fate.   His father would not have allowed idleness; he did not care about money-making, especially, but he did believe in work, for himself and his children. When the father died, and his son was left with enough money to have lived all his days without doing a stroke of work, he already had too much grit to think of such a life.   And he had too much good sense to start out to become a millionaire and to pile million upon useless million.

He had something else to fight against: bad health.   He writes: " I was a sickly, delicate boy, suffered much from asthma, and frequently had to be taken away on trips to find a place where I could breathe. One of my memories is of my father walking up and down the room with me in his arms at night, when I was a very small person, and of sitting up in bed gasping, with my father and mother trying to help me. I went very little to school. I never went to the public schools, as my own children later did." [1] For a few months he went to a private school, his aunt taught him at home, and he had tutors there.

When he was ten his parents took him with his brother and sisters for a trip to Europe, where he had a bad time indeed. Like most boys, he cared nothing for picture-galleries and the famous sights, he was homesick and he wished to get back to what really pleased him,— that is, collecting animals. He was already interested in that. And only when he could go to a museum and see, as he wrote in his diary, " birds and skeletons " or go " for a spree " with his sister and buy two shillings worth of rock-candy, did he enjoy himself in Europe.

His sister knew what he thought about the things one is supposed to see in Europe, and in her diary set it down:

" I am so glad Mama has let me stay in the butiful hotel parlor while the poor boys have been dragged off to the orful picture galary."

[1] " Autobiography."

These experiences are funny enough now, but probably they were tragic to kim at the time. In a church in Venice there were at least some moments of happiness. He writes of his sister " Conie " :

" Conie jumped over tombstones spanked me banged Ellies head &c."

But in Paris the trip becomes too monotonous; and his diary says:

November 26. " I stayed in the house all day, varying the day with brushing my hair, washing my hands and thinking in fact having a verry dull time."

November 27. " I did the same thing as yesterday."

They all came back to New York and again he could study and amuse himself with natural history. This study was one of his great pleasures throughout life and when he was a man he knew more about the animals of America than anybody except the great scholars who devoted their lives to this alone.

It started with a dead seal that he happened to find laid out on a slab in a market in Broadway. He was still a small boy, but when he heard that the seal had been killed in the harbor, it reminded him of the adventures he had been reading about in Mayne Reid's books. He went back to the market, day after day, to look at the seal, to try to measure it and to plan to own it and preserve it. He did get the skull, and with two cousins started what they gave the grand name of the " Roosevelt Museum of Natural History "!

Catching and keeping specimens for this museum gave him more fun than it gave to some of his family. His mother was not well pleased when she found some young white mice in the ice-chest, where the founder of the " Roosevelt Museum " was keeping them safe. She quickly threw them away, and her son, in his indignation, said that what hurt him about it was " the loss to Science! The loss to Science! " Once, he and his cousin had been out in the country, collecting specimens until all their pockets were full. Then two toads came along,— such novel and attractive toads that room had to be made for them. Each boy put one toad under his hat, and started down the road. But a lady, a neighbor, met them, and when the boys took off their hats, the toads did what any sensible toads would do, hopped down and away, and so were never added to the Museum.

The Roosevelt family visited Europe again in 1873, and afterwards went to Algiers and Egypt, where the air, it was hoped, would help the boy's asthma. This was a pleasanter trip for him, and the birds which he saw on the Nile interested him greatly.

His studies of natural history had been carried on in the summers at Oyster Bay on Long Island, on the Hudson and in the Adirondacks. They soon became more than a boy's fun, and some of the observations made when he was fifteen, sixteen or seventeen years old have found their way into learned books. When the State of New York published, many years afterwards, two big volumes about the birds of the state, some of these early writings by Roosevelt were quoted as important. A friend has given me a four-page folder printed in 1877, about the summer birds of the Adirondacks " by Theodore Roosevelt, Jr., and H. D. Minot." Part of the observations were made in 1874 when he was sixteen. Ninety-seven different birds are listed.

When he was fifteen and had returned a second time from Europe, he began to study to enter Harvard. He was ahead of most boys of his age in science, history and geography and knew something of German and French. But he was weak in Latin, Greek and mathematics. He loved the out-of-doors side of natural history, and hoped he might be a scientist like Audubon.

CHAPTER II

IN COLLEGE

ROOSEVELT entered the Freshman class of Harvard University in 1876. It is worth while to remember that this man who became as much of a Westerner as an Easterner, who was understood and trusted by the people of the Western States, was born on the Atlantic coast and educated at a New England college.

The real American, if he was born in the East, does not talk with contempt about the West; if he is a Westerner he does not pretend that all the good in the world is on his side of the Mississippi. Nor, wherever he came from, does he try to keep up old quarrels between North and South. Theodore Roosevelt was an American, and admired by Americans everywhere. Foolish folk who talk about the "effete East," meaning that the East is worn out and corrupt, had best remember that Abraham Lincoln did not believe that when he sent his son to the same college which Theodore Roosevelt's father chose for him.

At Harvard he kept up his studies and interest

in natural history. In the house where he lived
he sometimes had a large, live turtle and two or
three kinds of snakes. He went in to Boston and
came back with a basket full of live lobsters, to
the consternation of the other people in the horse-
car. He held a high office in the Natural History
Society, and took honors, when he graduated, in
the subject. His father had encouraged his desire to be a professor of natural history, remind-
ing him, however, that he must have no hopes of
being a rich man. In the end he gave up this
plan, not because it did not lead to money, for
never in his life did he work to become wealthy,
but because he disliked science as it was then
taught. One of the bad things the German universities had done to the American colleges was to
make them worship fussy detail, and so science
had become a matter of microscopes and labora-
tories. The field-work of the naturalist was
unknown or despised.

He took part in four or five kinds of athletics.
He seems never to have played baseball, perhaps
because of poor eyesight which made him wear
glasses. But he practiced with a rifle, rowed and
boxed, ran and wrestled. In his vacations he
went hunting in Maine. Boxing was one of his
favorite forms of sport,—for two reasons. He
thought a boy or a man ought to be able to de-

fend himself and others, and he enjoyed hard exercise.

It is important to know what he thought and did about self-defense and fighting. Many people dodge this, and other difficult subjects, when they are talking to boys. It was not Roosevelt's way to hide his thoughts in silence because of timidity, and then call his lack of action by some such fine name as " tact " or " discretion." When there was good reason for speaking out he always did so. Since a boy who is forever fighting is not only a nuisance, but usually a bully, some older folk go to the extreme and tell boys that all fighting is wrong.

Theodore Roosevelt did not believe it. When he was about fourteen, and riding in a stage-coach on the way to Moosehead Lake, two other boys in the coach began tormenting him. When he tried to fight them off, he found himself helpless. Either of them could handle him, could hit him and prevent him from hitting back. He decided that it was a matter of self-respect for a boy to know how to protect himself and he learned to box.

Speaking to boys he said later:

" One prime reason for abhorring cowards is because every good boy should have it in him to thrash the objectionable boy as the need arises."

And again:

"The very fact that the boy should be manly and able to hold his own, that he should be ashamed to submit to bullying, without instant retaliation, should in return, make him abhor any form of bullying, cruelty, or brutality." [1]

When he was teaching a Sunday School class in Cambridge, during his time at college, one of his pupils came in with a black eye. It turned out that another boy had teased and pinched the first boy's sister during church. Afterwards there had been a fight, and the one who tormented the little girl had been beaten, but he had given the brother a black eye.

"You did quite right," said Roosevelt to the brother and gave him a dollar.

But the deacons of the church did not approve, and Roosevelt soon went to another church.

Meanwhile he was learning to box. In his own story of his life he makes fun of himself as a boxer, and says that in a boxing match he once won "a pewter mug" worth about fifty cents. He is honest enough to say that he was proud of it at the time, "kept it, and alluded to it, and I fear bragged about it, for a number of years, and I only wish I knew where it was now."

[1] These two quotations from essay called "The American Boy" in "The Strenuous Life," pp. 162, 164.

His college friends tell a different story of him. He was never one of the best boxers, they say, and he was at a disadvantage because of his eyesight. But he was plucky enough for two, and he fought fair. He entered in the lightweight class in the Harvard Gymnasium, March 22, 1879. He won the first match. When time was called he dropped his hands, and his opponent gave him a hard blow on the face. The fellows around the ring all shouted "Foul! Foul!" and hissed. But Roosevelt turned toward them, calling "Hush! He didn't hear!"

In the second match he met a man named Charlie Hanks, who was a little taller, and had a longer reach, and so for all Roosevelt's pluck and willingness to take punishment, Hanks won the match.

He was a member of three or four clubs,— the Institute, the Hasty Pudding and the Porcellian. He was one of the editors of the *Harvard Advocate*, took part in three or four college activities, and was fond of target shooting and dancing. It is told that he never spoke in public, until about his third year in college, that he was shy and had great difficulty in speaking. It was by effort that he became one of the best orators of his day.

Roosevelt did not like the way college debates were conducted. He said that to make one side defend or attack a certain subject, without regard to whether they thought it right or wrong, had a bad effect.

" What we need," he wrote, " is to turn out of colleges young men with ardent convictions on the side of right; not young men who can make a good argument for either right or wrong, as their interest bids them."

He did one thing in college which is not a matter of course with students under twenty-two years old.   He began to write a history, named " The Naval War of 1812."   It was finished and published two years after he graduated, and in it he showed that his idea of patriotism included telling the truth.   Most American boys used to be brought up on the story of the American frigate *Constitution* whipping all the British ships she met, and with the notion that the War of 1812 was nothing but a series of brilliant victories for us.

Theodore Roosevelt thought that Americans were not so soft that they were afraid to hear the truth, and that it was a poor sort of American who dared not point out to his fellow-countrymen the mistakes they had made and the disasters which followed.   It did not seem patriotic to him to dodge the fact that lack of wisdom at Washington had let our Army run down before the war, so that our attempts to invade Canada were failures, and that we suffered the disgrace of having Washington itself captured and burned by the enemy.

There was a great deal to be proud of in what our Navy did, and in the Army's victory in the Battle of New Orleans, and these things Roosevelt described with the pride of every good American. But he had no use for the old-fashioned kind of history, which pretends that all the bravery is on one side. He did his best to get at the truth, and he knew that the English and Canadians had fought bravely and well, and so he said just that. Where our troops or our ships failed it was not through lack of courage, but because they were badly led, and what was worse, since it was so unnecessary, because the Government at Washington had lost the battle in advance by neglecting to prepare.

Before he was twenty-four, Roosevelt was so well-informed in the history of this period that he was later asked to write the chapter dealing with the War of 1812 in a history of the British Navy.

At his graduation from Harvard he stood twenty-second in a class of one hundred and seventy. This caused him to be elected to the Phi Beta Kappa, the society of scholars. Before he graduated he became engaged to be married to Miss Alice Lee of Chestnut Hill, Massachusetts.

He told his friend, Mr. Thayer, what he was going to do after graduation.

" I am going to try to help the cause of better government in New York City," he said. And he added :

" I don't know exactly how."

CHAPTER III

IN POLITICS

WHEN he graduated from college Roosevelt was no longer in poor health. His boxing and exercise in the gymnasium, and still more his outdoor expeditions, and hunting trips in Maine, had made a well man of him. He was yet to achieve strength and muscle, and his life in the West was to give him the chance to do that.

His father died while he was in college and he was left, not rich, but so well off that he might have lived merely amusing himself. He might have spent his days in playing polo, hunting and collecting specimens of animals. What he did during his life, in adding to men's knowledge of the habits of animals, would have gained him an honorable place in the history of American science, if he had done nothing else. So with his writing of books. He earned the respect of literary men, and left a longer list of books to his credit than do most authors, and on a greater variety of subjects. But he was to do other and

still more important work than either of these
things.

He believed in and quoted from one of the no-
blest poems ever written by any man,— Tennyson's " Ulysses." And in this poem are lines
which formed the text for Roosevelt's life:

> How dull it is to pause, to make an end,
> To rust unburnish'd, not to shine in use!
> As tho' to breathe were life.

This was the doctrine of " the strenuous life "
which he preached,— and practiced. It was to
perform the hard necessary work of the world,
not to sit back and criticize. It was to do disagreeable work if it had to be done, not to pick
out the soft jobs. It was to be afraid neither of
the man who fights with his fists or with a rifle,
nor of the man who fights with a sneering tongue
or a sarcastic pen.

To go into New York politics from 1880–1882
was, for a young man of Roosevelt's place in life,
just out of college, what most of his friends and
associates called " simply crazy." That young
men of good education no longer think it a crazy
thing to do, but an honorable and important one,
is due to Theodore Roosevelt more than to any
other one man.

As he sat on the window-seat of his friend's

room in Holworthy Hall, that day, and said he was going to try to help the cause of better government in New York, Mr. Thayer looked at him and wondered if he were " the real thing." Thirty-nine years later Mr. Thayer looked back over the career of his college mate, and knew that he had talked that day with one of the great men of our Republic, with one who, as another of his college friends says, was never a " politician " in the bad sense, but was always trying to advance the cause of better government.

The reason why it seemed to many good people a crazy thing to go into politics was that the work was hard and disagreeable much of the time. Politics were in the hands of saloon-keepers, toughs, drivers of street cars and other " low " people, as they put it. The nice folk liked to sit at home, sigh, and say: " Politics are rotten." Then they wondered why politics did not instantly become pure. They demanded " reform " in politics, as Roosevelt said, as if reform were something which could be handed round like slices of cake. Their way of getting reform, if they tried any way at all, was to write letters to the newspapers, complaining about the " crooked politicians," and they always chose the newspapers which those politicians never read and cared nothing about.

If any decent man did go into politics, hoping to do some good, these same critics lamented loudly, and presently announced their belief that he, too, had become crooked. If it were said that he had been seen with a politician they disliked, or that he ate a meal in company with one, they were sure he had gone wrong. They seemed to think that a reformer could go among other office-holders and do great work, if he would only begin by cutting all his associates dead, and refusing to speak to them.

It was a fortunate day for America when Theodore Roosevelt joined the Twenty-first District Republican Club, and later when he ran for the New York State Assembly from the same district. He was elected in November, 1881. This was his beginning in politics.

In the Assembly at Albany, he presently made discoveries. He learned something about the crooked politicians whom the stay-at-home reformers had denounced from afar. He found that the Assembly had in it many good men, a larger number who were neither good nor bad, but went one way or another just as things happened to influence them at the moment. Finally, there were some bad men indeed. He found that the bad men were not always the poor, the uneducated, the men who had been brought up in rough homes, lacking in refinement. On the contrary, he found some extremely honest and useful men who had had exactly such unfavorable beginnings.

Also, he soon discovered that there were, in and out of politics, some men of wealth, of education, men who boasted that they belonged to the " best families," who were willing to be crooked, or to profit from other men's crooked actions. He soon announced this discovery, which naturally made such men furious with him. They pursued him with their hatred all his life. Some people really think that great wealth makes crime respectable, and if it is pointed out to a wealthy but dishonest man, that he is merely a common thief, and if in addition, the fact is proved to everybody's satisfaction, his anger is noticeable.

Along with his serious work in the Assembly, Roosevelt found that there was a great deal of fun in listening to the debates on the floor, or the hearings in committees. One story, which he tells, is of two Irish Assemblymen, both of whom wished to be leader of the minority. One, he calls the " Colonel," the other, the " Judge." There was a question being discussed of money for the Catholic Protectory, and somebody said that the bill was " unconstitutional." Mr. Roosevelt writes:

The Judge, who knew nothing of the constitution, except that it was continually being quoted against all of his favorite projects, fidgetted about for some time, and at last jumped up to know if he might ask the gentleman a question. The latter said " Yes," and the Judge went on, " I'd like to know if the gintleman has ever personally seen the Catholic Protectoree?" " No, I haven't," said his astonished opponent. " Then, phwat do you mane by talking about its being unconstitootional? It's no more unconstitootional than you are!" Then turning to the house with slow and withering sarcasm, he added, " The throuble wid the gintleman is that he okkipies what lawyers would call a kind of a quasi-position upon this bill," and sat down amid the applause of his followers.

His rival, the Colonel, felt he had gained altogether too much glory from the encounter, and after the nonplussed countryman had taken his seat, he stalked solemnly over to the desk of the elated Judge, looked at him majestically for a moment, and said, " You'll excuse my mentioning, sorr, that the gintleman who has just sat down knows more law in a wake than you do in a month; and more than that, Mike Shaunnessy, phwat do you mane by quotin' Latin on the flure of this House, *when you don't know the alpha and omayga of the language!*" and back he walked, leaving the Judge in humiliated submission behind him.[1]

Another story also relates to the " Colonel." He was presiding at a committee meeting, in an extremely dignified and severe state of mind. He

[1] " American Ideals," p. 93.

usually came to the meetings in this mood, as a
result of having visited the bar, and taken a number of rye whiskies.   The meeting was addressed
by " a great, burly man . . . who bellowed as if
he had been a bull of Bashan."

The Colonel, by this time pretty far gone, eyed him
malevolently, swaying to and fro in his chair.   However, the first effect of the fellow's oratory was soothing
rather than otherwise, and produced the unexpected
result of sending the chairman fast asleep bolt up-
right.   But in a minute or two, as the man warmed up
to his work, he gave a peculiar resonant howl which
waked the Colonel up.   The latter came to himself with
a jerk, looked fixedly at the audience, caught sight of
the speaker, remembered having seen him before, for-
got that he had been asleep, and concluded that it must
have been on some previous day.   Hammer, hammer,
hammer, went the gavel, and —

" I've seen you before, sir ! "

" You have not," said the man.

" Don't tell me I lie, sir ! " responded the Colonel,
with sudden ferocity.   " You've addressed this committee on a previous day ! "

." I've never —" began the man ; but the Colonel
broke in again :

" Sit down, sir !   The dignity of the chair must be
preserved !   No man shall speak to this committee
twice.   The committee stands adjourned."   And with
that he stalked majestically out of the room, leaving
the committee and the delegation to gaze sheepishly into
each other's faces.[1]

[1] " American Ideals," p. 96.

There was in the Assembly a man whom Mr. Roosevelt calls " Brogan."

He looked like a serious elderly frog. I never heard him speak more than once. It was before the Legislature was organized, or had adopted any rules; and each day the only business was for the clerk to call the roll. One day Brogan suddenly rose, and the following dialogue occurred:

Brogan. Misther Clu-r-r-k!

The Clerk. The gentleman from New York.

Brogan. I rise to a point of ordher under the rules!

The Clerk. There are no rules.

Brogan. Thin I object to them.

The Clerk. There are no rules to object to.

Brogan. Oh! (nonplussed; but immediately recovering himself.) Thin I move that they be amended until there ar-r-re![1]

Roosevelt was three times elected to the Assembly. He took an interest in laws to reform the Primaries and the Civil Service, and he demanded that a certain corrupt judge be removed. This astonished the Assembly, for the judge had powerful and rich friends. His own party advised the twenty-three years old Assemblyman to sit down and shut his mouth. The judge might be corrupt, as it was charged, but it was " wiser " to keep still about it. Roosevelt, they said, was

[1] "Autobiography," p. 99.

" rash " and " hot-headed " to make trouble. And they refused to hear him.

But he got up next day, and the next, and the next after that, and demanded that the dishonest judge be investigated. And on the eighth day, his motion was carried by a vote of 104 to 6. The politicians saw to it that the judge escaped, but it was shown that Roosevelt's charges were true ones. And New York State found that she had an Assemblyman with a back-bone.

Roosevelt carried some bills for the cause of better government through the Assembly and they were signed by a courageous and honest Governor, named Grover Cleveland. Thomas Nast, America's great cartoonist of those days, drew a cartoon of the two men together. Cleveland was forty-four and Roosevelt was twenty-three.

One of the most important events while he was in the Assembly arose from a bill to regulate the manufacture of cigars in New York City. He had found that cigars were often made under the most unhealthy surroundings in the single living room of a family in a tenement. In one house which he investigated himself, there were two families, and a boarder, all living in one room, while one or more of the men carried on the manufacture of cigars in the same room. Everything about the place was filthy, and both for the

health of the families and of the possible users
of the cigars, it was necessary to have this state
of affairs ended.

He advocated a bill which passed, and was
signed by Governor Cleveland, forbidding such
manufacture. So far, so good; but there were
persons who found that the law was against their
interests. They succeeded in getting the Court
of Appeals to set the law aside, and in their
decision the judges said the law was an assault
upon the " hallowed associations " of the home!

This made Roosevelt wake to the fact that
courts were not always the best judges of the
living conditions of classes of people with whom
they had no contact. They knew the law; they
did not know life. The decision blocked tenement house reform in New York for twenty
years, and was one more item in Roosevelt's
political education.

CHAPTER IV

"RANCH LIFE AND THE HUNTING TRAIL"

AT the end of Mr. Roosevelt's membership in the New York Assembly, he began his life on a ranch in North Dakota. In this way he not only learned much about the Western people, but came to know the ranchman's life, and to have his first chance to shoot big game.

He had married Miss Lee in 1880, the autumn of the year he left college. Less than four years afterwards his wife died, following the birth of a daughter. His mother died on the next day, and Roosevelt under the sorrow of these two losses, left New York, and spent almost all his time on his ranch, the Elkhorn, at Medora.

The people in Dakota looked on this Eastern tenderfoot with a little amusement, and, at first, probably with some contempt. He was, to their minds, a "college dude" from the East, and moreover he wore eyeglasses. To some of the people whom he met, this fact, he says, was enough to cause distrust. Eyeglasses were under suspicion.

But, with two men who had been his guides in

Maine, Bill Sewall and Wilmot Dow, he began
his life as a ranchman and a cow-puncher, and
went through all the hard work and all the fun.
He took long rides after cattle, rounded them up
and helped in the branding. He followed the
herd when it stampeded in a thunderstorm. He
hunted all the game that there was in the county,
and also acted as Deputy Sheriff and helped
clear the place of horse-thieves and "bad men."

In one of his adventures Roosevelt showed that
he had taken to heart the celebrated advice which,
in Hamlet, Polonius gives to his son:

<blockquote>
Beware
Of entrance to a quarrel, but being in,
Bear't that the opposed may beware of thee.
</blockquote>

Mulvaney, in one of Kipling's stories, proved that
he knew something about Shakespeare, for he
put this advice into his own language so as to
express the meaning perfectly:

<blockquote>
"Don't fight wid ivry scutt for the pure joy av
fightin', but if you do, knock the nose av him first
an' frequint."
</blockquote>

Roosevelt tried to keep out of the fight,— but
this is the way it happened. He was out after lost
horses, and had to put up at a little hotel where
there were no rooms downstairs, but a bar, a

dining-room and a kitchen. It was late at night, and there was trouble on, for he heard one or two shots in the bar as he came up. He disliked the idea of going in, but it was cold outside and there was nowhere else to go. Inside the bar, a cheap " bad man " was walking up and down with a cocked revolver in each hand. He had been shooting at the clock, and making every one unhappy and uncomfortable.

When Roosevelt came in, he called him " Four eyes," because he wore spectacles, and announced " Four eyes is going to set up the drinks." Roosevelt tried to pass it off by laughing, and sat down behind the stove to escape notice, and keep away from trouble. But the " bad man " came and stood over him, a gun in each hand, using foul language, and insisting that " Four eyes " should get up and treat.

" Well," Roosevelt reluctantly remarked, " if I've got to, I've got to!" As he said this, he rose quickly, and hit the gun-man with his right fist on the point of the jaw, then with his left, and again with his right. The guns went off in the air, as the " bad man " went over like a nine-pin, striking his head on the corner of the bar as he fell. Roosevelt was ready to drop on him if he moved, for he still clutched the revolvers. But he was senseless.

The other people in the bar recovered their nerve, once the man was down. They hustled him out into the shed, and there was no more trouble from him.

Roosevelt hunted geese and ducks, deer, mountain sheep, elk and grizzly bear during his stay in the West. It was still possible to find buffalo, although most of the great herds had vanished. The prairie was covered with relics of the dead buffalo, so that one might ride for hundreds of miles, seeing their bones everywhere, but never getting a glimpse of a live one. Yet he managed, after a hard hunt of several days, to shoot a great bull buffalo.

An encounter with a grizzly bear is much more exciting, and he was nearly killed by one bear. In later years Roosevelt killed almost every kind of large and dangerous game that there is on the earth,— lions, elephants, the African buffalo, and the rhinoceros. The Indian tiger is perhaps the only one of the large savage animals which he never encountered. Yet after meeting all these and having some close shaves, especially with a wounded elephant in Africa, he said that his narrowest escape was with this grizzly bear.

It was when he had returned to the West and was on a hunt in Idaho. He had had trouble with his guide, who got drunk, so they parted company, and Roosevelt was alone. Looking down into a valley, from a rocky ridge, he saw a dark object, which he discovered was a large grizzly bear. He fired, and the bear giving a loud grunt, as the bullet struck, rushed forward at a gallop into a laurel thicket. Roosevelt paused at the edge of the thicket and peered within, trying to see the bear, but knowing too much about them to go into the brush where he was.

When I was at the narrowest part of the thicket, he suddenly left it, directly opposite, and then wheeled and stood broadside to me on the hillside, a little above. He turned his head stiffly towards me; scarlet strings of froth hung from his lips; his eyes burned like embers in the gloom.

I held true, aiming behind the shoulder, and my bullet shattered the point or lower end of his heart, taking out a big nick. Instantly the great bear turned with a harsh roar of fury and challenge, blowing the bloody foam from his mouth, so that I saw the gleam of his white fangs; and then he charged straight at me, crashing and bounding through the laurel bushes, so that it was hard to aim. I waited until he came to a fallen tree, raking him as he topped it with a ball, which entered his chest and went through the cavity of his body, but he neither swerved nor flinched, and at the moment I did not know that I had struck him. He came steadily on, and in another second was almost upon me. I fired for his forehead, but my bullet went

Courtesy of Charles Scribner's Sons.

THEODORE ROOSEVELT WHEN ABOUT
10 YEARS OLD

low, entering his open mouth, smashing his lower jaw and going into the neck. I leaped to one side almost as I pulled the trigger; and through the hanging smoke the first thing I saw was his paw as he made a vicious side blow at me. The rush of his charge carried him past. As he struck he lurched forward, leaving a pool of bright blood where his muzzle hit the ground; but he recovered himself and made two or three jumps onwards, while I hurriedly jammed a couple of cartridges into the magazine, my rifle holding only four, all of which I had fired. Then he tried to pull up, but as he did so his muscles seemed suddenly to give way, his head drooped, and he rolled over and over like a shot rabbit. Each of my first three bullets had inflicted a mortal wound.[1]

There were, once, near Mr. Roosevelt's ranch, three men who had been suspected of cattle-killing and horse-stealing. The leader was a tall fellow named Finnegan, who had long red hair reaching to his shoulders, and always wore a broad hat and a fringed buckskin shirt. He had been in a number of shooting scrapes. The others were a half-breed, and a German, who was weak and shiftless rather than actively bad. They had a bad reputation, and were trying to get out of the country before the Vigilance Committee got them.

About the only way to travel — it was early in March and the rivers were swollen — was by

[1] "The Wilderness Hunter," pp. 305-6.

boat down the river. So when the cowboys on Mr. Roosevelt's ranch found that his boat was stolen, they were sure who had taken it. As it is every man's duty in a half-settled country to bring law-breakers to justice, and as Roosevelt was, moreover, Deputy Sheriff, he decided to go after the three thieves. Two of his cow-boys, Sewall and Dow from Maine, in about three days built another boat. In this, with their rifles, food enough for two weeks, warm bedding and thick clothes, Roosevelt, Sewall and Dow set out down the Little Missouri River.

There had been a blizzard, the weather was still bitterly cold, and the river full of drifting ice. They shot prairie fowl and lived on them, with bacon, bread and tea. It was cold work poling and paddling down the river, with the current, but against a head wind. The ice froze on the pole handles. At night where they camped the thermometer went down to zero. Next day they shot two deer, for they needed meat, as they were doing such hard work in the cold.

On the third day they sighted smoke,— the camp-fire of the three thieves. Two boats, one of them the stolen one, were tied up to the bank. It was an exciting moment, for they expected a fight. As it turned out, however, it was a tough job, but not a fighting one. The German was

alone in camp, and they captured him without
trouble. The other two were out hunting.
When they came back an hour or two later, they
were surprised by the order to hold up their
hands. The half-breed obeyed at once, Finni-
gan hesitated until Roosevelt walked in close,
covering him with a rifle, and repeated the command. Then he gave up.

But this was only the beginning of a long,
hard task. It was often the way to shoot such
men at once, but Sheriff Roosevelt did not like
that. He was going to bring them back to jail.
At night the thieves could not be tied up, as they
would freeze to death. So Roosevelt, Sewall and
Dow had to take turns in watching them at night.
After they started down river again, they found
the river blocked by ice, and had to camp out for
eight days in freezing weather. The food all but
gave out, and at last there was nothing left but
flour. Bread made out of flour and muddy water
and nothing else, is not, says Mr. Roosevelt, good
eating for a steady diet. Besides they had to be
careful of meeting a band of Sioux Indians, who
were known to be in the region.

At last they worked back to a ranch, borrowed
a pony, on which Roosevelt rode up into the
mountains to a place where there was a wagon.
He hired this, with two broncos and a driver.

Sewall and Dow took the boats down the river, while Roosevelt set out on a journey which took two days and a night, walking behind the wagon, and guarding the three men.   The driver of the wagon was a stranger.

At night they put up at a frontier hut, and the Deputy Sheriff had to sit up all night to be sure the three prisoners did not escape.   When he reached the little town of Dickinson, and handed the men over to the Sheriff, he had traveled over three hundred miles.   He had brought three outlaws to justice, and done something for the cause of better government in the country where he lived.

CHAPTER V

TWO DEFEATS

ALTHOUGH he was still under twenty-five when he left the New York Assembly, Roosevelt was favorably known throughout the State. He had been heard of, by those who keep up with politics, all over the country. In 1884, the year of a Presidential election, he was one of the four delegates-at-large from New York to the Republican convention at Chicago. The leader for the Presidential nomination was James G. Blaine, a brilliant man who had many warm admirers. Also, there were many in his own party, who distrusted him, who thought that in the past he had not been strictly honest. Good men differed on this question and differ still.

Roosevelt favored Senator Edmunds of Vermont, but he had agreed beforehand, with other young Republican delegates, that they would support for the election the man named by the convention. Since, in later years, Roosevelt refused to abide by the decision of a party convention, and led one of the most extraordinary " bolts " in the history of American politics, it is important to consider for a moment the question of political parties and the attitude a man may take toward them.

Because parties are responsible for a good many small, mean, and sometimes dishonorable acts, we often hear parties and partisanship denounced. People express the wish that there might be an end to " party politics " and to " partisanship," and that " all good men might get together " for the good of the whole country. This may happen when there is Heaven on earth, but not before. Even the good and honest men continue to differ about which is the wisest way to do things, and so the people who think the same way about most matters get together in a party. The suggestion, by the way, that people should give up " partisan-ship " often comes from people who do not by any means intend to give up their own partisanship,— they wish other folk to come over to their own way of thinking. We are all apt to wish that others would only be reasonable enough to agree with *us*.

Nor is it at all sure that everything would be fine if there were no parties. Countries which have tried to do without parties, have not made a great success of it. There must be some organized group to hold responsible if men in office do

badly; some people to warn that the things they
are doing are not approved by the majority of the
people.

With parties in existence, as they have been for
almost all of our history as a nation, there are in
the main, four ways in which a man may act
toward them.   He may be a hidebound party man,
always voting the party ticket, and swallowing the
party platforms whole.   Such persons often get
into the newspapers when they are elderly, as having voted for every candidate on this or that party
ticket for fifty or sixty or seventy years.   It
simply means, of course, that these men are proud
of the fact that they let other people do their thinking for them.

Or, a man may look upon a party as the means
through which he may secure better government.
He is proud of its wise and good acts, and is willing to forgive its mistakes, because he knows that
no large group of men can be perfect.   He be-
lieves in remaining loyal to his party as long as
possible, but he does not set it above his country,
nor agree to follow it when it goes absolutely
wrong, or falls into the hands of men who hold
party welfare above patriotism.   Roosevelt was a
party man of this kind.

Furthermore, a man may be an Independent,
one who will not join any party for long.   Many

of these are highly honorable and wise citizens, who are of great value to the country, although they can usually be nothing but helpers in any good cause. Their position nearly always prevents their becoming the chief actors in bringing about any good and desirable reform.

The fourth class in which a man may find himself in regard to parties, is that of the so-called independent, who mistakes his own fussiness for nobility of character. He can find fault with everybody and every party, but he can be loyal to none. He is strong on leaving a party for the smallest excuse; never on staying with it. It is as if a member of a foot-ball team, half an hour before the game, should refuse to play, because some other member of the team had once cheated in an examination. He satisfies his own conscience, but he fails in the loyalty he owes to the team and its friends.

At the convention in 1884 Roosevelt took an important part for so young a man. He made speeches and worked for Senator Edmunds, but Mr. Blaine was nominated. This caused a split in the party, and many of its members joined the Democrats. They were called by their opponents " Mugwumps," and since they believed they were acting for the best, they did not mind being called that or any other name.

So many prominent and able Republicans joined the Mugwumps it is sometimes forgotten that many more equally good and wise Republicans refused to " bolt," but stayed with the party and voted for Mr. Blaine. Either they did not at all believe the charges which had been made against him — and it is as impossible now as it was then to prove the charges — or else they thought that the country would be far worse off with the Democratic party in power than with the Republicans successful.

Mr. Roosevelt was disgusted with the result of the convention, but did not believe that he was justified in leaving the party. He therefore stayed in it, and supported Mr. Blaine.

The Democrats nominated the courageous Governor of New York, Grover Cleveland. Both before and after this, he and Mr. Roosevelt worked together for measures of good government, and respected each other, while belonging to different parties. The presidential election turned out to be close, and in the end several incidents besides the split in the Republican party worked against Blaine. He was narrowly defeated. The change of a few hundred votes in the State of New York would have made Blaine the President. As in later years large election frauds were discovered to have been going on in New York, some people contend with good show of reason, that Blaine and not Cleveland was really the choice of the voters.

Two years after this, in 1886, when Roosevelt was on his Dakota ranch, the Republicans nominated him for Mayor of New York City. He was about twenty-eight years old, and it is evident that he had made a mark in politics. He came East, accepted the nomination, and made the campaign.

The opponents were, first, Abram S. Hewitt, a respectable candidate nominated by Tammany Hall in its customary fashion of offering a good man, now and then, to pull the wool over the eyes of persons who naturally need some excuse for voting to put New York into the hands of the political organization whose existence has always been one of America's greatest disgraces.

The other candidate was Henry George, a man of high character, nominated by the United Labor Party. Mr. Hewitt was elected, with Mr. George second and Mr. Roosevelt third.

About a month after the election, Mr. Roosevelt went to England, where he married Miss Edith Kermit Carow, of New York. She had been his friend and playmate when he was a boy, and was his sister's friend. The groomsman was a young Englishman, Mr. Cecil Spring-Rice. Years later the groom and his " best man " came together

again in Washington, when the American was
President Roosevelt, and the Englishman was Sir
Cecil Spring-Rice, the British Ambassador to the
United States.

CHAPTER VI

FIGHTING OFFICE-SEEKERS

To tell the story of Roosevelt's life it is necessary to talk much about politics, and that to some people is a dull subject. But he was in political office over twenty years of his life, always interested and active in politics, and the vigor which he brought to his duties made public affairs attractive to thousands of Americans who had felt little concern about them.

This alone was a great service. If a man is going the wrong way in political life, if he is trying to do unwise or evil things, he is a danger, but a danger which may be corrected. He may be made to turn his efforts in useful directions. But the man who takes no interest at all in the government of his city, state or nation, who is so feeble that he cannot even take the time to vote on election day, but goes hunting or fishing instead, — this man is a hopeless nuisance, who does not deserve the liberty which he enjoys, nor the protection which his government gives him.

Politics, when Mr. Roosevelt was active, were

not dull.   Few men have ever made them so lively and interesting.   Every activity in life meant something to him, a chance for useful work or for good fun.   He had a perfectly " corking time," he said, when he was President, and the words shocked a number of good people who had pardoned or overlooked dirty actions by other public men, so long as these other men kept up a certain copy-book behavior which they thought was " dignity."

It is a question if any man ever had a better time, ever had more real fun in his life, than did Mr. Roosevelt.   In spite of the hard work he put in, in spite of long days and weeks of drudgery he knew how to get happiness out of every minute. He did not engage in drinking and gambling for his amusements.   He did not adopt a priggish attitude on these matters,— he simply knew that there were other things which were better sport. He was a religious man, a member all his life of his father's church, but religion did not sour him, make him gloomy, or cause him to interfere with other people about their belief or lack of it.

He got an immense amount of pleasure in his family life, in half a dozen kinds of athletic sports, especially the ones which led him outdoors, and in books.   In these things he was marvelously wise or marvelously fortunate.   Some men's lives are spent indoors, in an office or in a study among books. Their amusements are indoor games, and they come to despise or secretly to envy, the more fortunate men who live outdoors.

Some of the outdoors men, on the other hand, become almost as one-sided. Knowing nothing of the good fun that is in books they deny themselves much pleasure, and take refuge in calling "high-brows" the men who have simply more common sense and capacity for enjoyment than themselves.

Mr. Roosevelt, more than most men of his time, certainly more than any other public man, could enjoy to the utmost the best things the world has in it. He knew the joy of the hard and active life in the open, and he knew the keen pleasure of books. So when he returned to America after his marriage in 1886, he built a house on Sagamore Hill at Oyster Bay on Long Island. Here he could ride, shoot, row, look after his farm, and here in the next year or two he wrote two books. One was the life of Gouverneur Morris, American minister to France in the early years of our nation; the other a life of Senator Thomas H. Benton of Missouri.

But he was not long to stay out of political office. In 1888 President Cleveland had been defeated for reëlection by the Republican candidate,

Benjamin Harrison.   The new President appointed Mr. Roosevelt as one of the Civil Service Commissioners, with his office in Washington.

Most politicians are charged, certainly Mr.
Roosevelt was sometimes charged, with being a
selfish seeker after personal advancement.   There
is not much on which to base this argument in
Mr. Roosevelt's acceptance of this office.   For the
man who is looking out merely for his own ambitions, for his own success in politics, is careful of
the position he takes, careful to keep out of offices
where there are many chances to make enemies.
The Civil Service Commission was, of all places
at that time, the last where a selfish politician
would like to be.   Nobody could do his duties
there and avoid making enemies.   It was a thankless job, consisting of trying to protect the public
interests against a swarm of office-seekers and
their friends in Congress.

It is ridiculous now to remember what a fight
had to be waged to set up the merit system of the
Civil Service in this country.   The old system,
by which a good public servant was turned out to
make room for a hungry office-seeker of the successful political party, was firmly established.
Men and women were not appointed to office because they knew anything about the work they
were to do, but because they were cousins of a

Congressman's wife, or political heelers who had helped to get the Congressman elected. Nobody thought of the offices as places where, for the good of the whole country, it was necessary to have the best men. Instead, the offices were looked on as delicious slices of pie to be grabbed and devoured by the greediest and strongest person in sight.

The Civil Service Commission, when Mr. Roosevelt became a member, had been established by Congress, but it was hated and opposed by Congress and the Commission was still fought, secretly or openly. Congressmen tried to ridicule it, to hamper it by denials of money, and to overrule it in every possible way. A powerful Republican Congressman and a powerful Democratic Senator tried to browbeat Roosevelt, and were both caught by him in particularly mean lies. Naturally they did not enjoy the experience.

At the end of his term, President Harrison was defeated by Mr. Cleveland, who came back again to the Presidency. He re-appointed Mr. Roosevelt, who thus spent six years in the Commission. When he retired he had made a good many enemies among the crooked politicians, and some friends and admirers among well-informed men who watch the progress of good government. He was still unknown to the great body of cit-

Mr. Roosevelt as a Hunter in his Ranching Days

izens throughout the country, although he had been fighting their fight for six years.

He went from Washington to accept another thankless and still more difficult position in New York City.   It was one which had been fatal to political ambitions, and was almost certain to end the career of any man who accepted it.   This was the Presidency of the Board of Police Commissioners.

CHAPTER VII

POLICE COMMISSIONER

EXPERIENCED politicians always warn young men who wish to rise in politics, who wish to hold high office in the state or national government, to keep out of city politics. It is a grave-yard for reputations, and it was that in 1895, when Roosevelt took charge of the New York Police, even more than to-day.

Between the unreasonable reformers, who expect perfection, arrived at in their own way; the sensible folk who demand an honest government; the lax and easy-going people who do not care how much rottenness there is about, so that it is kept partly covered up (and this is one of the largest classes) and the plain criminals who are out for graft and plunder, the city office-holder is torn in a dozen ways at once.

If he is dishonest or weak, he goes under immediately. If he is honest, but lacking in perfect courage, he is nearly useless. And if he is both honest and brave, but has not good brains, is not able to use his mind quickly and well, he is either helpless, or soon placed in a position where he seems to have been dishonorable. For, of course the first method which a crooked man uses to destroy his honest opponent, is to try to make him look crooked, too. Often during his life Roosevelt insisted upon the fact that a man in public life must not only be honest, but that he must have a back-bone and a good head into the bargain.

Nothing but a sense of public duty, nothing but a desire to help the cause of better government, could have made a man take the Police Commissionership in 1895. Mayor Strong, on a Reform ticket, had beaten Tammany Hall. He wanted an able and energetic man and so sent for Roosevelt. The condition of the Police Department sounds more like a chapter from a dime novel gone mad, than from any real state of things which could exist in a modern city. Yet it did exist.

The police were supposed to protect the city against crime. What they really did was to stop some of the crime — when the criminal had no " pull "— and to protect the rest of it. The criminal handed over a certain amount of his plunder to the police, and they let him go on with his crime. More than that, they saw that no one bothered him. There was a regular scale of prices for things varying all the way from serious crime down to small offenses. It cost more to be a highway robber, burglar, gun-man or murderer, for instance, than merely to keep a saloon open after the legal time for closing. A man had to pay more for running a big gambling-house, than simply for blocking the side-walk with rubbish and ash-cans.

Roosevelt found that most of the policemen were honest, or wished to be honest. But, surrounded as they were by grafters, it was almost impossible for a man to keep straight. If he began by accepting little bribes, he ended, as he rose in power, by taking big ones, and finally he was in partnership with the chief rascals. The hideous system organized by the powerful men in Tammany Hall spread outward and downward, and at last all over the city. Roosevelt did not stop all the crime, of course, nor leave the city spotless when he ended his two years service. But he did make it possible for one of his chief opponents, one of the severest of all critics, Mr. Godkin, a newspaper editor, to write him, at the end of his term of office:

"In New York you are doing the greatest work of which any American to-day is capable, and exhibiting to the young men of the country the spectacle of a very important office administered by a man of high

character in the most efficient way amid a thousand
difficulties. As a lesson in politics, I cannot think of
anything more instructive." [1]

How did he do this? First, he tried to keep
politics out of the police-force,— to appoint men
because they would make good officers, not because they were Republicans or Democrats.
Next, he tried to reward and promote policemen
who had proved themselves brave,— who had
saved people in burning houses or from drowning,
or had arrested violent men at great danger to
themselves. This is commonly done in the New
York Police Department to-day: it was not so
common before 1895. Roosevelt and his fellow
commissioners found one old policeman who had
saved twenty-five people from drowning and two
or three from burning buildings. They gave him
his first promotion. He began to have the Department pay for a policeman's uniform when it
was torn in making an arrest or otherwise ruined
in the performance of duty. Before, the policeman had had to pay for a new uniform himself.
He had each policeman trained to use a pistol, so
that if he had to fire it at a criminal, he would hit
the criminal, and not somebody else. He did his
best to stop the custom of selling beer and whiskey

[1] Thayer, "Theodore Roosevelt," p. 106.

to children.   Finally he stopped disrespect for
law by having law enforced, whether people liked
it or not.

Of course, this got him into hot water.   One of
our worst faults in America lies in passing a tremendous number of laws, and then letting them be
broken.   In many instances the worst troubles are
with laws about strong drink.   People in the State,
outside of New York City, and some of those in
the City, wished to have a law to close the saloons
on Sunday.   So they passed it.   But so few people in the City really wished such a law, so many
of them wished to drink on Sunday, that the
saloons stayed open, and the saloon-keepers paid
bribes to the police for " protection."   The result
was not temperance, but the opposite.   Moreover
it led to disrespect for the law, and corruption for
the police.   It was not Commissioner Roosevelt's
business whether the law was a wise one or not,
but it was his business to enforce it.

He enforced it, and had the saloons closed.   As
he said : " The howl that rose was deafening.   The
professional politicians raved.   The yellow-press
surpassed themselves in clamor and mendacity.
A favorite assertion was that I was enforcing a
' blue law,' an obsolete law that had never before
been enforced.   As a matter of fact, I was en-

forcing honestly a law that had hitherto been enforced dishonestly." [1]

In the end, those who wished to drink on Sun-
days found a way to do it, and the law intended
to regulate drinking habits failed, as such laws
nearly always have done. A judge decided that
as drink could be served with meals, a man need
only eat one sandwich or a pretzel and he could
then drink seventeen beers, or as many as he liked.
But the result of Roosevelt's action had nearly
stopped bribe-giving to the police. So there was
something gained.

Roosevelt went about the city at night, sometimes alone, sometimes with his friend Jacob Riis,
a reporter who knew about police work and the
slum districts of the city. If he caught policemen off their beat, they were ordered to report at
his office in the morning and explain. When his
friends were dancing at fashionable balls, he was
apt to be looking after the police outside.

From about this time, Roosevelt began to be
known all over the United States. He had been
heard of ever since he was in the Assembly, but
only by those who follow politics closely. Now,
New York newspapers, with their cartoons, began
to make him celebrated everywhere. The fact

[2] "Autobiography," p. 210.

that when he spoke emphatically, he showed his teeth for an instant, was enlarged upon in pictures and in newspaper articles, and it became connected with him henceforth.

We demand amusing newspapers; we like the fun in every subject brought out as no other nation does. And we get it. Our newspapers are by far the brightest and most readable in the world. But we have to pay for it, and we often pay by having the real truth concealed from us in a mass of comedy. Newspapers seize upon a man or woman who has something amusing in his life, manner, or speech, and play upon that peculiarity until at last the true character of the person is hidden.

This happened with Roosevelt. About the time of his Police Commissionership, the newspaper writers and artists began to invent a grotesque and amusing character called " Teddy," who was forever snapping his teeth, shouting " Bully!" or rushing at everybody, flourishing a big stick. This continued for years and was taken for truth by a great many people. To this day, this imaginary person is believed in by thousands. And in the meantime, the genuine man, a brave high-minded American, loving his country ardently, and serving her to the utmost of his great strength and ability, was engaged in his work, known by all who had personal contact with him to be stern indeed against evil-doers, but tender and gentle to the unfortunate, to women and children and to animals.

CHAPTER VIII

THE ROUGH RIDER

In 1897 the Republican Party came again into power; Mr. McKinley was inaugurated as President. Roosevelt was appointed Assistant Secretary of the Navy, and came with his family to Washington. The Secretary of the Navy was Mr. John D. Long.

America was within a year of getting into war, and as usual was not ready for it. There are men so foolish as to rejoice because we have never been ready for the wars in which we have taken part about every twenty or thirty years in our history. This simply means that they rejoice at the unnecessary deaths of thousands of other Americans who die from disease in camp, or are killed in the field through neglect to prepare in advance. Preparation for war is not wholly the matter of having weapons ready to fight the enemy. It also means healthy camps for our soldiers to live in, and readiness to furnish clothing, food and medical supplies. For lack of these, thousands of our

58

friends and relatives die in every war we are in.

A rebellion had been going on in Cuba for years. The cruel government of Spain had kept the Cubans in misery and in rebellion, and disturbed the friendship between Spain and the United States. It was our duty to see that Cuban expeditions did not sail from our coast to help their friends, and in this work a great many ships of our Navy were busy all the time. Nobody liked to have to do this for we naturally sympathized with the Cubans, who were making such a brave fight against stupid and tyrannical governors sent from Spain. One of the last of these was particularly bad. He herded the Cuban people into camps where they died of disease and starvation, and he had great numbers of them shot without mercy. We had justly revolted against the misgovernment of King George III in 1776, but nothing that King George's governors and generals had done to us was as bad as the things the Spaniards were doing in Cuba, in 1896 and 1897.

Many of the men in Washington felt that war would come sooner or later. Roosevelt believed it and worked constantly to have the Navy ready. He had the support of the President and of Secretary Long in nearly everything that he proposed, and so was able to do some useful work. It is important to understand what Roosevelt thought about war, not only about this, but about all wars. Here it is in his own words.

I abhor unjust war. I abhor injustice and bullying by the strong at the expense of the weak, whether among nations or individuals. I abhor violence and bloodshed. I believe that war should never be resorted to when, or so long as, it is honorably possible to avoid it. I respect all men and women who from high motives and with sanity and self-respect do all they can to avert war. I advocate preparation for war in order to avert war; and I should never advocate war unless it were the only alternative to dishonor.[2]

You will be able to see from what he did while he was President, when he was in a position where he could have plunged the country into war half a dozen times, whether these words were true, or whether he was really the fire-eater which some of his enemies insisted he was.

He secured from Congress nearly a million dollars, to permit the Navy to engage in target-practice. To those who were alarmed at such "waste," he remarked that gun-powder was meant to be burned, and that sailors must learn to shoot, since in battle, the shots that hit are the only ones that count. There is nothing wonderful about such remarks. In looking back at them

[1] "Autobiography," p. 226.

there seems to be nothing wonderful about many things that he said and did. They are merely examples of plain, common-sense, and it appears ridiculous that anybody should have had to make such remarks, or to fight hard to get such clearly necessary things done. Yet he did have to fight for them. It had to be driven into the heads of some of the men in Congress that it is not the proper use of gun-powder to keep it stored up, until war is declared, then bring it out, partly spoiled, and give it to soldiers and sailors, who for lack of practice, do not know how to shoot straight.

Roosevelt also was able to help in having appointed to command the Asiatic squadron, a naval officer named Commodore George Dewey.

On February 15, 1898, while affairs were at their worst between America and Spain, our battleship *Maine* was blown up in Havana Harbor. She had gone there on a friendly visit, but now was destroyed and sent to the bottom. Over two hundred and fifty of our men were killed. Almost every one knew that war was now certain. For weeks the country debated as to the cause of the explosion which sank the *Maine,* and the matter was investigated by naval officers assisted by divers. They found that the explosion had come

from the outside. Somebody had set off a mine
or torpedo beneath the ship. Nobody in America
disputed this, except a few of the peace-at-any-
price folk, who preferred to think that the care-
lessness of our own sailors had been the cause.
These gentlemen always think the best of the people of other nations, which is a fine thing; but
they are always ready to believe the worst of their
own countrymen, which is, on the whole, rather a
nasty trait.

Roosevelt worked at top-speed in the Navy Department, and began to lay plans for going to the
war himself. He believed that it was right and
necessary to fight Spain, and end the horrible suffering in Cuba. And he believed that it was the
duty first and foremost of men like himself, who
advised war, to take part in it. He was nearly
forty years old, and had a family. Many other
men in his place would have discovered that their
services were most important in Washington.
They would have stayed in their offices, and let
other men (whom they called " jingoes ") do the
fighting for them. It was never Roosevelt's custom to act that way.

Later in February, while Mr. Long was away,
and Roosevelt was Acting-Secretary of the Navy,
he sent this cable message to Commodore
Dewey:

Washington, February 25, '98.

Dewey, Hong Kong

Order the squadron, except the *Monocacy,* to Hong Kong. Keep full of coal. In the event of declaration of war Spain, your duty will be to see that the Spanish squadron does not leave the Asiatic coast, and then offensive operations in Philippine Islands. Keep *Olympia* until further orders.

Roosevelt.

War against Spain was declared in April,— the month in our history which has also seen the beginning of our Revolution, our Civil War, and our entrance into the Great War against Germany. Congress arranged for three regiments of volunteer cavalry to be raised among the men in the Rockies and on the Great Plains who knew how to ride and shoot. Here Roosevelt saw his chance. He knew these men and longed to go to war in their company.

The Secretary of War offered to make him Colonel of one of these regiments. It is worth while to notice what his reply was. He knew how to manage a horse and a rifle, he had lived in the open and could take care of himself in the field. He had had three years in the National Guard in New York, rising to the rank of Captain. Many men in the Civil War without one half of his experience and knowledge, gayly accepted Brigadier-Generalships. Also, in the Spanish War, another public man, Mr. William J. Bryan, allowed himself to be made a Colonel, and took full command of a regiment, without one day's military experience. Yet Roosevelt declined the offer of a Colonel's commission and asked to be made Lieutenant-Colonel, with Leonard Wood, of the regular Army as his Colonel.

When you hear or read that Roosevelt was a conceited man, always pushing himself forward, it may be well to ask if that is the way a conceited man would have acted.

Colonel Wood was an army surgeon, who had been a fighting officer in the campaign against the Apaches. He had been awarded the Medal of Honor, the highest decoration an American soldier can win for personal bravery.

The new regiment, the First United States Volunteer Cavalry, was promptly called, by some newspaper or by the public, the " Rough Riders," and by that name it is always known. Most of the men in it came from Arizona, New Mexico, Oklahoma and the Indian Territory, but it had members from nearly every State. Many Eastern college men were in it, including some famous foot-ball players, polo-players, tennis champions and oarsmen. The regiment trained at San Antonio, and landed in Cuba for the attack on Santiago on June 22. The troopers had to leave their horses behind, so they were to fight on foot after all. Roosevelt's Rough Riders, somebody said, had become Wood's Weary Walkers. The walking was not pleasant to some of the cow-boys, who never used to walk a step when there was a horse to ride.

Within a day or two they were in a fight at Las Guasimas. It was a confusing business, advancing through the jungle and fired at by an enemy they could not see. The Rough Riders lost eight men killed and thirty-four wounded. The Spaniards were using smokeless powder, then rather a new thing in war. Two of our regiments at Santiago were still using black powder rifles, and the artillery used black powder, which by its smoke showed the enemy just where they were. Our artillery was always silenced or driven off, because this country had been so neglectful of its Army and its men as to let poor, old backward Spain get better guns, and more modern ammunition than ours. That never should happen with a rich, progressive country like ours.

A few days later came the fight at San Juan. Colonel Wood had been put in command of the brigade, so Roosevelt led the regiment of Rough Riders. It was a fearfully hot day; many men dropped from exhaustion. The regular regiments of cavalry, together with the Rough Riders, all fighting on foot, moved forward against the low hills on which were the Spaniards in block-houses or trenches. For some while they were kept waiting in reserve, taking what shelter they could from the Mauser bullets, which came whirring through the tall jungle grass. This is the most trying part of a fight. It is all right when at last you can charge your enemy and come to close quarters with him, but to lie on the ground under fire, unable to see anybody to fire upon, is the worst strain upon the soldiers' nerves. As one after another is shot, the officers begin to watch the men closely to see how they are standing it. Roosevelt received a trifling wound from a shrapnel bullet at the beginning of the fight. Later his orderly had a sun-stroke, and when he called another orderly to take a message, this second man was killed as he stood near, pitching forward dead at Roosevelt's feet.

Finally came the order to charge. Roosevelt was the only mounted man in the regiment. He had intended to go into the fight on foot, as he had at Las Guasimas, but found that the heat was so bad that he could not run up and down the line and superintend things unless he was on horseback. When he was mounted he could see his own men better, and they could see him. So could the enemy see him better, and he had one or two narrow escapes because of being so conspicuous.

He started in the rear of the regiment, which is where the Colonel should be, according to the books, but soon rode through the lines and led the charge up " Kettle Hill,"— so-called by the Rough Riders because there were some sugar kettles on top of it.   His horse was scraped by a couple of bullets, as he went up, and one of the bullets nicked his elbow.   Members of the other cavalry regiments were mingled with the Rough Riders in the charge,— their officers had been waiting for orders, and were glad to join in the advance. The Spaniards were driven out and the Rough Riders planted their flags on the hill.

But there were other hills and other trenches full of Spaniards beyond, and again the Rough Riders, mixed with men of other regiments, went forward.   In cleaning out the trenches Roosevelt and his orderly were suddenly fired on at less than ten yards by two Spaniards.   Roosevelt killed one of them with his revolver.   The Rough Riders had had eighty-eight killed and wounded out of less than five hundred men who were in the fight.

The American forces were now within sight of Santiago, but they had to dig in and hold the ground they had taken.   There was a short period in the trenches, which seemed tedious to the riders from the plains, but was nothing to what men, years later, had to endure in the Great War against Germany. At last Santiago surrendered, on July 17.

The war ended within about a month. Commodore Dewey had beaten the Spanish Fleet at Manila and Admiral Sampson and his fleet had destroyed the Spanish cruisers which were forced out of Santiago Harbor on July 3rd, as a result of the Army getting within striking distance of the city. One other thing of importance was done by Roosevelt before the regiment was brought home to Montauk Point and mustered out. After the surrender of Santiago it was supposed that the war was going on and that there would be a campaign in the winter against Havana. But the American Army was full of yellow fever. Half the Rough Riders were sick at one time, and the condition of other regiments was as bad. The higher officers knew that unless the troops were taken to some healthier climate to recover, there would be nothing left of them. Over four thousand men were sick, and not ten per cent. of the Army was fit for active work. But the War Department would not listen to the suggestion that the army be sent for a while to a cooler climate.

What none of the regular Army officers could afford to do, Roosevelt did. He wrote a letter to

General Shafter, the commander of the expedition, explaining the state of things, and setting out how important it was, if any of the army was to be kept alive, that they should be sent away from Cuba, until the sickly season was over. General Shafter really wished such a letter to be written, and he allowed the Associated Press reporter to have it as soon as it was handed to him.

Then, all the Generals joined with Roosevelt in a " Round Robin " to General Shafter, saying the same things. The Government at Washington began to take notice, and in a short time ordered the army home.

Roosevelt had taken a leading part in an act which caused him to be severely blamed by many, to be denounced by all who worship military etiquette, and charged with " insubordination " by men who would rather make a mess of things and do it according to the rules of the book, than succeed in something useful and do it by common-sense rules made up at the time. He had shocked the folks who like red tape, and he had helped save the lives of perhaps four thousand men.

CHAPTER IX

WHEN the Rough Riders were disbanded at Montauk Point in September 1898, Theodore Roosevelt was the most popular man in America. This is the judgment of his best historian, Mr. Thayer, and it is undoubtedly correct. The war had made known to the country a number of professional soldiers or sailors — especially Admiral Dewey and Admiral Sampson, whose conduct had been splendid. It had also created some popular " heroes," whose fame was brief. But Colonel Roosevelt was first and foremost a *citizen,* his career as a soldier was for a few months only. Behind that was a solid foundation of service in civil office. Ahead of it were still finer achievements, also in civil life. He felt the pride which all men feel — despite much pretense and humbug — to have had the chance to lead men in battle for a just cause, to have put his life in danger when his country needed such offer of sacrifice.

But the Santiago campaign, the charge up San

Juan hill, did not "make" Roosevelt. It was a dramatic episode in his history; it attracted attention to him. Such are the peculiar conditions of politics, it proved a short cut to the White House. He said, frankly, that he would never have been President if the Rough Riders had not gone to Cuba. In this he underestimated himself, as he often did. He had too much ability in politics, too much courage in fighting for the cause of better government, at a time when courage was badly needed, to have failed to rise to the highest office. Back in the days when he was Civil Service Commissioner two visitors in the White House, saw him, also a visitor, looking about the rooms.

" There is a young man," said one of them, who knew him, " who is going to move into this house himself, before long."

After Cuba, the next step was the Governorship of New York State. Before he was out of uniform, the politicians began talking about him for the place. The Republican party in New York was in a bad way. They had quarreled among themselves; the Democrats had just beaten them in an election. They knew they must have a strong candidate for Governor, or the Democrats, (that is, Tammany Hall) would get control at Albany.

This was the great day of the political Bosses. Perhaps at no time since have they been quite as powerful as they were then. A man named Croker was the Boss of the Democratic Party; a man named Platt, the Boss of the Republicans. Men called the Boss of their own party the " Leader," but they referred to the " Leader " of the other party as the Boss, without wasting any politeness. Most men do not pay much attention to politics; a Boss is a man who pays too much attention to them. He exists because the average citizen thinks he has done his whole duty if he votes on election day. A Boss works at his business, which is politics, night and day, all the year round. He might be very useful if he could be kept honest. He manages to get a great deal of power, in ways that are shady, if not actually criminal. Then, if he is one kind of a Boss, greedy for money, he sells this power to the highest bidder. Men are nominated for office, because the Boss has picked them out, as a poultryman might select a fat goose. Usually he selects a man who will obey orders. But another kind of Boss does not especially care for money. He likes the power which his position gives him, he likes to be able to move men about as if they were toy-soldiers.

Such apparently was Senator Platt, the Republican Boss of New York. People had so neglected their duty of managing their own af-

fairs in politics, that he had seized the reins, and
could say who should be nominated.   In the same
way Croker was the ruler of the Democratic party
in New York, and could say who should be nominated in his party.

Now, in such a situation, what was an honest
man to do?   The best men in the Republican party
believed that Roosevelt was the only one who
could be elected, that the people believed so firmly
in his honor and courage that they would vote for
him.   Senator Platt did not want him, did not
like him, but he came to see that they could win
with him, and with no one else.   So Roosevelt
was nominated, and elected, by a narrow lead of
18,000 votes.   So far, the people could rule with
Roosevelt as their servant.   But the Governor can
do little alone; he must have the support of the
Legislature and the other State officers.   The
Boss hoped to rule through them, to say who
should be appointed to office, to decide which bill
should pass and which be defeated.

There were people who would have had Governor Roosevelt declare war on Platt; refuse to have
anything to do with him; refuse even to speak to
him.   In that way he could have done nothing for
the good of the State; he could have spent his
term in fighting Platt, made a great show of independence and reform, but, in point of fact, ad-

vanced the cause of good government not an inch. All of his proposals would have been blocked by Platt's men in the Legislature.

Instead, he acted in accord with the facts as they were; not as if they were the way he would have liked them to be. If Platt could not rule he could ruin. So the Governor treated him politely, and only disagreed with him when the Boss proposed something actually bad. For instance, there was a most important officer, the Superintendent of Public Works, to be appointed. Senator Platt informed Governor Roosevelt that a certain man had been chosen; he showed him the telegram with the man's acceptance. Roosevelt said, quietly, something like this:

" I think not, Senator. The Governor appoints that officer, and I am the Governor."

Platt was very angry; Roosevelt refused to get angry, but stuck to his decision, and made his own choice. Things like this happened again and again, during the two years while Roosevelt was Governor of New York.

Every honorable man in American politics has to fight against this evil of the Boss. Officeholders, Presidents and Governors, come and go, but the Bosses hold their power for a long time. So long as they exist it is not wise for us to talk

too much about Kings and their tyranny.   For a
Boss is very like a King.   Platt and Croker
thought that the people were not fit to rule; theirs
was much the same idea that King George the
Third and the German Kaiser had.   The best and
wisest men have had to admit the strength of the
Boss and try to deal with him as well as they
could; Abraham Lincoln even had to appoint one
to his Cabinet.   The Boss creeps into power while
the people are asleep.

Roosevelt pointed out that it is not hard for a
man to be good if he lives entirely by himself.
Nor is it difficult for him to get things done, if he
is careless about right and wrong.   The hard
thing, yet the one which must be demanded of the
public man, is to get useful things done, and to
keep straight all the while.   When Roosevelt was
elected Governor, John Hay, the Secretary of
State, wrote to him:

"You have already shown that a man may be absolutely honest and yet practical; a reformer by instinct
and a wise politician; brave, bold and uncompromis-
ing, and yet not a wild ass of the desert.   The exhibi-
tion made by the professional independents in voting
against you for no reason on earth except that somebody else was voting for you, is a lesson that is worth
its cost." [1]

[1] "Autobiography," p. 296.

The year 1900 was the year of a Presidential election.   Mr. McKinley was to run again on the Republican ticket, and later it appeared that Mr. Bryan would oppose him again, as he had in 1896. The Republican Vice-President, Mr. Hobart, had died in office, so the Republicans had to find someone to go on the ticket with President McKinley. Roosevelt was mentioned for the office, and Platt warmly agreed, hoping to get him out of New York politics.   Roosevelt, at first, refused to consider an office which has more dignity than usefulness about it.   Another utterance of Secretary of State John Hay is interesting.   He wrote to a friend:

"Teddy has been here: have you heard of it? It was more fun than a goat. He came down with a somber resolution thrown on his strenuous brow to let McKinley and Hanna know once for all that he would not be Vice-President, and found to his stupefaction that nobody in Washington, except Platt, had ever dreamed of such a thing." [1]

Mr. Hay was one of the wisest of our statesmen; one of the most polished and agreeable men in public life. Yet this letter shows how the older men often mistook Roosevelt. For, in less than a year after Mr. Hay had gently poked fun at "Teddy" for thinking that he might

[1] Thayer, p. 148.

be made Vice-President, and said that there was
not the slightest danger of such a thing happening,
Roosevelt had been elected to that office.   His enjoyment of his work, his bubbling merriment, his
lack of the old-fashioned, pompous manners which
used to be supposed proper for a statesman, made
many older men inclined to treat him with a sort
of fatherly amusement.   They looked at his acts
as an older man might look at the pranks of a boy.
And then, suddenly, they found themselves serving
under this "youngster," in the Government!   It
was a surprise from which they never recovered.

I have said that the reporters, the makers of
funny pictures in the newspapers, and others, ex-
aggerated Roosevelt's traits, and created a false
idea about him.   This is true.   But it is also true
that there was a great deal of real and honest fun
poked at him throughout his life, and that it added
to the public enjoyment of his career.   The
writers of comic rhymes, the cartoonists, and the
writers of political satire had a chance which no
other President has ever given them.   Many of
our Presidents — wise and good men — and
many Senators, Governors, Cabinet officers and
others, have gone about as if they were all ready
to pose for their statues.   Roosevelt never did
this.   He bore himself in public with dignity, and
respect for the high offices to which the people

elected him. But he did not suggest the old style of portrait, in which a statesman is standing stiffly, hand in the breast of his coat, a distant view of the Capitol in the background. He had too keen a sense of fun for anything of the sort.

Nobody laughed at the jokes about him more heartily than he did himself. When " Mr. Dooley " described his adventures as a Rough Rider, and spoke of him as " Alone in Cubia," as if he thought he had won the war all by himself, he wrote to the author:

" Three cheers Mr. Dooley ! Do come on and let me see you soon. I am by no means so much alone as in Cubia. . . ."

" Let me repeat that Dooley, especially when he writes about Teddy Rosenfelt has no more interested and amused reader than said Rosenfelt himself." [1]

Mr. McKinley was re-elected President of the United States and Mr. Roosevelt was elected Vice-President in November 1900. Roosevelt had taken part in the campaign before election, and of this Mr. Thayer writes:

He spoke in the East and in the West, and for the first time the people of many of the States heard him speak and saw his actual presence. His attitude as a

[1] Scribner's Magazine, December, 1919, p. 658.

speaker, his gestures, the way in which his pent up
thoughts seemed almost to strangle him before he could
utter them, his smile showing the white rows of teeth,
his fist clenched as if to strike an invisible adversary,
the sudden dropping of his voice, and leveling of his
forefinger as he became almost conversational in tone,
and seemed to address special individuals in the crowd
before him, the strokes of sarcasm, stern and cutting,
and the swift flashes of humor which set the great
multitude in a roar, became in that summer and
autumn familiar to millions of his countrymen; and
the cartoonists made his features and gestures familiar
to many other millions.[1]

In the following March he was sworn in as
Vice-President.   His duties as presiding officer of
the Senate were not severe, and he went on a
cougar hunt in Colorado in the winter before in-
auguration to enable him to bear the physical in-
activity of his new work.

When he came back to Washington again, to
hold the second highest place in the national government, it troubled him to think that he had
never finished the study of law, begun in New
York many years before.   He asked his friend,
Justice White of the Supreme Court, if it would
be wrong for him to take a legal course in a
Washington law school.   The Justice told him
that it would hardly be proper for the Vice-Presi-

[1] Thayer, p. 51.

dent to do that, but offered to tutor him in law. They agreed to study together the following winter.

But Roosevelt's term as Vice-President was coming to an end. He only occupied the office for six months. He was soon to succeed to the highest office of all.

PRESIDENT ROOSEVELT SPEAKING IN ALABAMA

CHAPTER X

In the first week of September 1901, President McKinley was killed by an anarchist in Buffalo. The young man who shot him was rather weak-minded, and had been led to believe, by the speeches and writings of others, craftier and wickeder than himself, that he could help the poor and unfortunate by murdering the President. This he treacherously did while shaking hands with him.

One of the leaders of the poisonous brood who had made this young man believe such villainous nonsense was a foreign woman named Emma Goldman, who for twenty or thirty years went up and down the land, trying to overthrow the law and government, yet always calling for the protection of both when she was in danger. The American Government tolerated this mischief-maker until 1919, when it properly sent her, and others of her stripe, back to their own country.

President McKinley, who was the gentlest and kindest of men, did not die immediately from the

bullet wound, but lingered for about a week.
Vice-President Roosevelt joined him in Buffalo,
and came to believe, from the reports of the doctors, that the President would get well. So he
returned to his family who were in the Adirondacks. A few days later, while Mr. Roosevelt
was mountain-climbing, a message came that the
President was worse and that the Vice-President
must come at once to Buffalo. He drove fifty
miles by night, in a buckboard down the mountain
roads, took a special train, and arrived in Buffalo
the next afternoon.

Mr. McKinley was dead, and Theodore Roosevelt took the oath of office as President. He was
under forty-three years of age, the youngest man
who had ever become President.

It is important to note his first act. It
was to insist that all of Mr. McKinley's Cabinet
remain in office. Thus he secured for the continued service of the Nation, some of its ablest
men: Mr. Hay, one of the most accomplished Sec-
retaries of State we have ever had, and Mr. Root,
Secretary of War, and afterwards Secretary of
State, whose highly trained legal mind placed him
at the head of his profession.

A test of a great man, as well as a test of a
modest man, in the true sense, is whether he is
willing to have other able and eminent men

around him as his assistants and fellow-workers. The most remarkable instances of this among our Presidents were Washington and Lincoln. The latter appointed men not because they admired him, or were personally agreeable to him; indeed some of his strongest and bitterest antagonists were put in his Cabinet, because he knew that they could well serve the country.

Mr. McKinley had chosen excellent Cabinet officers, and these Mr. Roosevelt kept in office, promoting them and appointing other men of high ability to other offices as the need arose. He did not care to shine as a great man among a group of second-rate persons; he preferred to be chief among his peers, the leader of the strongest and most sagacious of his time.

In saying this, I do not mean to compare Roosevelt with Washington or Lincoln or any of the noble figures of the past. Such comparisons are made too often; every President for fifty years has been acclaimed by his admirers as " the greatest since Lincoln," or " as great as Lincoln." This is both foolish and useless. There has been no character in our land like Lincoln; he stands alone. What we can say of Mr. Roosevelt, now, is that he was admired and beloved by millions of his fellow-countrymen while he lived; that his was an extraordinary and entirely different char-

acter from that of any of our Presidents; and
that upon his death thousands who had opposed
him and bitterly hated him but a few years before,
were altering their opinion and speaking of him
in admiration — with more than the mere respect
which custom pays to the dead. This has gone
on, and other unusual signs have been given of
the world's esteem for him. So much we can say;
and leave the determination of his place in our
history for a later time than ours.

One thing which many people feared when
Roosevelt became President was that he would get
the country into a war. They thought he liked
war for its own sake. Men said: "Oh! this
Roosevelt is such a rash, impulsive fellow! He
will have us in a war in a few months!" The
exact opposite was the truth. He kept our country and our flag respected throughout the world;
he avoided two possible wars; he helped end a foreign war; we lived at peace. Of him it can truly
be said: he kept us out of war, and he kept us in
the paths of honor.

He preached the doctrine of the square deal.

" A man who is good enough to shed his blood
for his country, is good enough to be given a
square deal afterward. More than that no man is
entitled to, and less than that no man shall have." [1]

[1] Springfield, Ill., July 4, 1903.   Thayer, p. 212.

He did not seek help and rewards from the rich by enabling them to prey upon the poor; neither did he seek the votes and applause of the poor by cheap and unjust attacks upon the rich. To the people who expect a public man to lean unfairly to one side or the other; who cannot understand any different way of acting, he was a constant puzzle.

" Oh! we have got him sized up!" they would say, " he is for the labor unions against the capitalist!" and in a few months they would be puzzled again: " No; he is for Wall Street and he is down on the poor laboring man."

For a long time they could not get it into their heads that he was for the honest man, whether laboring man or capitalist, and against the dishonest man, whether laboring man or capitalist.

" While I am President the doors of the White House will open as easily for the labor leader as for the capitalist,— *and no easier.*" [1]

Many Presidents might have said the first part of that sentence. Few of them would have added the last three words.

He annoyed many people in the South by inviting a very able and eminent Negro, Booker T. Washington, to eat luncheon with him. According to the curious way of thinking on this subject,

[1] Hagedorn, p. 242.

Mr. Washington who had been good enough to eat dinner at the table of the Queen of England, was not good enough to eat at the White House. Shortly after being violently denounced for being too polite to a Negro, he was still more violently denounced for being too harsh to Negroes. He discharged from the Army some riotous and disorderly Negro soldiers. Persons with small natures had attacked him for showing courtesy to a distinguished man; other persons with equally small natures now attacked him for acting justly towards mutinous soldiers.

What did he do while he was President? What laws were passed by Congress, which he advocated or urged, and which he approved by his signature? Here are some of them as they are given by Mr. Washburn,[1] a Congressman of that time:

The Elkins Anti-Rebate Law, to end unjust business dealings of the railroads.

The creation of the Department of Commerce and Labor.

The law for building the Panama Canal.

The laws to prevent impure and poisonous food being sold under false labels; and the law to establish the proper inspection of meat.

The creation of the Bureau of Immigration.

The law limiting the working hours of em-

[1] Washburn, "Theodore Roosevelt," p. 128.

ployees and protecting them in case of injury in
their occupations.

The law against child-labor in the District of
Columbia.

The reformation of the Consular Service.

The law to stop corporations from giving great
sums of money for political purposes at election
time.

You will notice that these were not laws to
enable a few rich men to get richer still at the
expense of the many; neither were they designed
to help dishonest labor leaders to plunder the em-
ployers. They were aimed to bring about justice
between man and man, to protect the weak.

There was, when Mr. Roosevelt became President, a long standing dispute between this country
and England and Canada about the boundary of
Alaska. This was quickly settled by arbitration;
our rights were secured; and all possible causes of
war were removed.

The South American country, Colombia, made
an attempt to block the building of the Panama
Canal. This canal had been planned to run
through the State of Panama, which was part of
the Republic of Colombia. It was a part of that
country, however, separated by fifteen days' journey from the capital city, Bogotá, and so separated in friendship from the rest of the country

that it had made over fifty attempts in fifty years
to revolt and gain independence.   Our State Department, through Mr. Hay, had come to an understanding with the Minister from Colombia as
to the canal, and the amount we were to pay
Colombia for the privilege of building this important waterway, for the benefit of the whole
world.

But the Colombian Government at that time
were a slippery lot,— dealing with them, said
President Roosevelt, " was like trying to nail cur-
rant jelly to a wall."   It struck them that they
would do well to squeeze more money yet out of
Uncle Sam, and that they might by twisting and
turning, get forty million dollars as easily as ten
millions.   So they delayed and quibbled.

In the meantime, the people of Panama, not
wishing to lose the advantage of the canal, and
desiring greatly to take any opportunity to free
themselves from the Colombians who had plun-
dered them for years, declared a revolution, which
took place without bloodshed.   Colombian troops,
coming to try to reconquer Panama, were for-
bidden to land by our ships, acting under President Roosevelt's orders.   We were under treaty
agreement to preserve order on the Isthmus.   Our
Government recognized the new Republic of Panama, an act which was promptly followed by all

the nations of the earth.   We then opened negotiations with Panama, paid the money to her, and
built the Canal.

Of course the politicians in Colombia gave vent
to a piercing howl.   A tricky horse-dealer, who
has a horse which he has abused for years, but
desires to sell to a customer for four times its
value, would be angry if the horse ran away, and
he lost not only the animal, but also his chances of
swindling the customer.   So with the Colombians.
Some people in this country took up their cry, and
professed to feel great sorrow for Colombia.   It
was noticed, however, that this sorrow seemed to
afflict most pitifully the people who were strongest
in their opposition to Mr. Roosevelt, and this
caused a suspicion that their pretended horror at
the act of our Government was not so much based
upon any knowledge of the facts, as upon a readiness to think evil of the President.   Others who
joined in an expression of grief at the time, and
later attempted to bolster up Colombia's claims
for damages, belonged to that class referred to in
connection with the sinking of the *Maine,* who always think the best of any foreign country and
suspect the worst of their own.

The fact that other countries instantly recognized Panama, and that President Roosevelt's action was completely and emphatically endorsed by

Secretary Hay, proved that the Panama incident was an example of the promptness, wisdom and courage in the conduct of foreign relations which leads alike to justice and the satisfactory settlement of difficult problems. For not the bitterest opponent of Mr. Roosevelt's administration ever dared to cast a shadow of doubt upon the honesty of Secretary Hay. The canal is now built, thanks in large part to President Roosevelt, and we have had a chance to see that wise decisions may often be reached swiftly; whereas dawdling, hesitation and timidity, which are sometimes mistaken for statesmanship, are more than apt to end, not only in general injustice, but in practical failure.

The war between Russia and Japan took place during President Roosevelt's term of office. After it had been going on over a year, and Japan had won victories by land and sea, the President asked both countries to open negotiations for peace. He continued to exert strong influence in every quarter to help bring the two enemies to an agreement. Only since his death has it become generally known how hard he worked to this end. A peace conference was held at Kittery Navy Yard in Maine, and a treaty was signed which ended the war.

For his action in this, President Roosevelt was the first American to receive the Nobel Peace

Prize. This was a sad reverse to the predictions of those who had been so sure that he was longing to start wars, instead of end them. Indeed, men who prophesied evil about Mr. Roosevelt, as well as those who tried to catch him in traps, had a most disappointing experience. The Nobel Prize consisted of a diploma, and an award in money of $40,000. This he tried to devote to helping the cause of peace between capital and labor in America. When Congress failed to take the needed action to apply his money for this purpose, it was returned to him. During the Great War he gave all of it to different relief organizations, like the Red Cross, and other societies for helping the sufferers.

The President assembled the most powerful fleet we had ever had together, sixteen battleships, with destroyers, and sent them on a cruise around the world. This was bitterly opposed at the time. Public men and newspapers predicted that the fleet could never make the voyage, or that even if it could, its effect would be to cause war with some other nation. The most emphatic predictions were made by a famous newspaper that the entrance of the fleet into the Pacific Ocean would be the signal for a declaration of war upon us by a foreign power. Nothing of the sort happened. The cruise attracted to the American navy the admiration of the world; it immensely increased the usefulness of the Navy itself by the experience it gave the officers and men; and it served warning upon anybody who needed it (and some folk did need it) that America was not a country of dollar-chasing Yankees, rich and helpless, but that it had the ability to defend itself.

This was an illustration of Roosevelt's use of the old saying: " Speak softly and carry a big stick; you will go far." When he first repeated this, it was seized upon by the newspapers for its amusing quality, and he was henceforth pictured as carrying a tremendous bludgeon, of the sort which giants usually bore in the tale of " Jack the Giant Killer." Timid folk thought that it proved their worst fears about his fondness for a fight. They failed to notice the " Speak softly " part of the saying. It was only a vivid way of advising his countrymen to be quiet and polite in their dealings with other nations, but not to let America become defenseless. What hasty and shallow critics denounced as the threat of a bully, proved in practice to be the sagacious advice of a statesman, whose promise when he took office, to preserve the peace and honor of his beloved country, was kept faithfully and precisely.

And he was able to keep the peace, to fill the office of President for seven years without having a shot fired by our forces, because he made it clear that this country would not submit to wrong, would not argue or bicker with foreign trespassers, kidnappers, highwaymen or murderers, but would promptly fight them. He did not fill the air with beautiful words about his love of peace; but we had peace. For as he knew perfectly well, there were countries, like Canada, with which we could live at peace for a hundred years and more, without needing forts or guns between them and us, because we think alike on most subjects, and respect each other's honor.

And there were other countries, Germany in particular, against whom all her neighbors have to live armed to the teeth, and in deadly fear, because the Germans respect nothing on earth except force. To argue or plead with the Germans, as he well knew, was not only a waste of time, it was worse: it was a direct invitation to war. Because since 1870 the Germans think that any country which professes to love peace, any country whose statesmen utter noble thoughts about peace, is simply a cowardly country, bent on making money, and afraid to fight. So when,— during Roosevelt's administration, the biggest swaggering " gun-man " of the world, the Kaiser Wilhelm of Germany, made a threat against the peace of America, Roosevelt no more read him pretty lectures about his love of peace, than he would have recited poetry to that other gun-man in the hotel in Dakota years before. He simply told the Kaiser in a few words, just what would happen if Germany didn't drop it. It was so quietly done that nobody knew anything at all about it until years afterward. There was no delay; there was no endless note-writing; there was no blustering; the Kaiser climbed down; *and there was no war*.

This, I am inclined to think, was one of the most important events of Roosevelt's seven years in the White House. If we wish America to live henceforth in peace and in honor, there is no incident of the past thirty years which should be studied by every American with more care. Germany began her attack on the world long before 1914. She bullied here, and she schemed and plotted there, but she was at work for years. In 1898 she tried to range the countries of Europe against us, as we went to war with Spain. England stood our friend and kept her off. Germany sent a fleet meddling into Manila Harbor to annoy and threaten Admiral Dewey. He refused to be frightened by them however and as an English squadron which was also there played the part of a good friend, the German admiral had his trip for nothing.

Later, about a year after Mr. Roosevelt became

President, the German Kaiser discovered a way, as he thought, to grab some territory in South America. Our Monroe Doctrine, which insures peace in the Western Hemisphere, by forbidding European nations to seize land here, was an obstacle to the Kaiser. He disliked it. But taking as pretext the fact that some people in Venezuela owed money to various Europeans, including Germans, he induced England and Italy to join in sending a fleet for a blockade of the Venezuelan coast. The English and Italians agreed, before long, to arbitrate their difficulty with Venezuela, and moreover they had no intention of seizing land. The German plan was quite different. They threatened to bombard Venezuelan towns, and we know enough now of their methods to say that they were hoping for something which might serve as an excuse for landing troops and taking possession of towns and territory. This was in defiance of our Monroe Doctrine; it aimed at setting up an Emperor's colonies in South America, and putting the peace of both South and North America into danger. Mr. Roosevelt did not mean to allow it.

But consider the situation. Germany was the foremost military power of the world. Her army was almost the greatest; probably the best trained and equipped. Ours was one of the smallest. Germany was not engaged in difficulties elsewhere.

She faced us across no barriers but the sea. No great French and British armies held the lines against her, as they did in later years when once more she threatened America. No mighty British fleet held the seas and kept the German Navy cooped up where it could do no harm,— except to such merchant ships, passenger steamers and hospital boats as it could strike from under the water. We faced Germany alone. But we had two means of defense. One of them was Admiral Dewey and his ships. The first of them, however, and the only one needed, was the cool-headed and brave-hearted man in the White House.

He told the German Ambassador, quietly and without bluster, that unless the Kaiser agreed to arbitrate his quarrel with Venezuela, and unless he agreed within a short time, ten days or less, Admiral Dewey would be ordered to Venezuela to protect it against a German attack. The German ambassador said that, of course, as the All Highest Kaiser had refused once before to arbitrate, there could be nothing done about it. All Highests do not arbitrate. People simply have to step aside.

President Roosevelt informed the German Ambassador that this meant war. A few days later when the German Ambassador was again at the White House, the President asked if the Kaiser had changed his mind. The Ambassador seemed

Courtesy of Charles Scribner's Sons.

THE ROUGH RIDER

With Mr. Punch's best wishes to Colonel Roosevelt, President of the United States.

(A Cartoon in *Punch* when Colonel Roosevelt became President.)

to think that it was a joke.   The Kaiser change
his mind at the bidding of a Yankee President!
It was almost funny!

"All right," said President Roosevelt, "I can
change my mind.   Admiral Dewey will not even
wait until Tuesday to start for Venezuela.   He
will go on Monday.   If you are cabling to Berlin,
please tell them that."

The pompous Ambassador was much flustered.
He hurried away, but returned in about a day and
a half, still out of breath.

"Mr. President," he said, "His Imperial
Majesty the Emperor has agreed to arbitrate with
Venezuela."

So there was no delay, no long and distressing
argument; and there was no war.   The President
could do this because he knew his countrymen; he
knew that they were not cowards.   He knew they
never had failed to back up their leader in the
White House.   He knew that no President need
worry about loyalty when he tells America that a
foreign enemy is making threats.   He has seen his
courageous predecessor, Grover Cleveland, rouse
America, as one man, over another Venezuelan
incident, a dozen or more years before.   And he
knew that the only occasion when America had
ever seemed about to fall into doubt and hesitation
in time of danger, was when that doubt and

hesitation began in the White House,— in the administration of Buchanan, before the Civil War. America will always support her President, if war threatens,— but America expects him to show leadership. Timidity in the leader will make timidity in the nation.

So the Kaiser changed his mind and gave in,— why? Because he knew that there was a President in the White House whose words were easy to understand; they did not have to be interpreted nor explained. And moreover, when these words were uttered, the President would make them good, every one.

CHAPTER XI

THE LION HUNTER

OTHER important events of President Roosevelt's administration will best be described farther on. For their importance increased after he was out of office, and they had a great influence upon a later campaign.

Here, it should be said that in 1904, as the term for which he was acting as Mr. McKinley's successor, drew toward an end, he was nominated by the Republican Party to succeed himself. There was some talk of opposition within his party, especially from the friends of "big business" who thought that he was not sufficiently reverent and submissive to the moneyed interests. This opposition took the form of a move to nominate Senator Hanna. But the Senator died, and the talk of opposition which was mostly moonshine, faded away.

When the campaign came in the autumn of 1904, his opponent was the Democratic nominee, Judge Parker, also from New York. Mr. Roosevelt was elected by a majority of more than two million and a half votes,— the largest majority ever given to a President in our history, either before or since that time.

On the night of election day he issued a statement in which he said: " Under no circumstances will I be a candidate for or accept another nomination." Of this he writes:

The reason for my choice of the exact phraseology used was twofold. In the first place, many of my supporters were insisting that, as I had served only three and a half years of my first term, coming in from the Vice-Presidency when President McKinley was killed, I had really had only one elective term, so that the third term custom did not apply to me; and I wished to repudiate this suggestion. I believed then (and I believe now) the third term custom or tradition to be wholesome, and therefore, I was determined to regard its substance, refusing to quibble over the words usually employed to express it. On the other hand I did not wish simply and specifically to say that I would not be a candidate for the nomination in 1908, because if I had specified the year when I would not be a candidate, it would have been widely accepted as meaning that I intended to be a candidate some other year; and I had no such intention, and had no idea that I would ever be a candidate again. Certain newspaper men did ask me if I intended to apply my prohibition to 1912, and I answered that I was not thinking of 1912, nor of 1920, nor of 1940, and that I must decline to say anything whatever except what appeared in my statement.[1]

[1] "Autobiography," pp. 422–3.

From March 4, 1905, until March 4, 1909, he was an elected President, not a President who had succeeded to the office through the death of another. When the end of his term approached he threw his influence in favor of the nomination of Mr. William H. Taft, Secretary of War in his Cabinet. He could have had the nomination himself if he had wished it; indeed he had to take precautions against being nominated. But Mr. Taft was nominated, and in November, 1908, was elected over Mr. Bryan, who was then running for the Presidency for the third time.

President Roosevelt and President-elect Taft drove up Pennsylvania Avenue to the Capitol together, March 4, 1909, in a cold gale of wind, which had followed a sudden blizzard. The weather was an omen of the stormy change which was coming over the friendship of these two men. An hour or two later it was President Taft who drove back to the White House, while Mr. Roosevelt, once more a private citizen, was hurrying to his home in Oyster Bay, to get ready for his hunting trip to Africa.

This was the vacation to which he had been looking forward for years. He had long been a friend of a number of famous hunters, and had corresponded with and received visits from some of them. Chief among these was Mr. Frederick Selous, one of the greatest of African hunters. Those who have read any of Rider Haggard's fine stories of adventure (especially " King Solomon's Mines " and " Allan Quartermain ") will be interested to know that Mr. Selous was the original of Quartermain. Adventures like these of Selous, the opportunity to see the marvelous African country, and the chance to shoot the dangerous big game, made Roosevelt long to visit Africa.

So he headed a scientific expedition sent out by the Smithsonian Institution to collect specimens for the National Museum at Washington. With him went his son Kermit, a student at Harvard; and three American naturalists. They left America only two or three weeks after his term as President had ended, and they came out of the African wilderness at Khartoum about a year later. With friends whom they met in Africa, English and American hunters, and a long train of native bearers and scouts, they visited the parts of Africa richest in game, and killed lions, leopards, hyenas, elephants, rhinoceros, hippopotamus, zebra, giraffe, buffalo, and dozens of other kinds of animals. Mr. Roosevelt and Kermit shot about a dozen trophies for themselves; otherwise nothing was killed which was not intended as a

museum specimen or for meat.   No useless butch-
ery of animals was allowed; often at great incon-
venience and even danger, animals were avoided
or driven off rather than let them be killed need-
lessly.   Some of the finest groups of mounted
animals in the country are now standing in the
National Museum, as a result of this trip.

They saw many wonderful sights.   They saw
a band of Nandi warriors, fierce savages, naked,
and armed only with shields and long spears, attack and kill a big lion.   Kermit Roosevelt took
photographs of most of the large game, coming
up to close quarters in order to get his pictures.
He took two or three photographs of a herd of
wild elephants in the forest, going at great risk
within twenty-five yards of the herd to be sure to
get a good view.

One day's hunting, which Mr. Roosevelt de-
scribes, shows what the country was like, how full
it was of all kinds of animals.   Leaving camp at
seven in the morning they were out altogether over
fifteen hours.   They were after a lion, so did not
look for other game.   They soon passed some
zebra, and antelope, but left them alone.   The
country was a dry, brown grassland, with few
trees, and in some places seems to have looked like
our Western prairie.   At noon they sighted three
rhinoceros, which they tried to avoid, as they did

not wish to shoot them.   Of course, in such circumstances it is necessary to do nothing to disturb the temper of the animals — stupid, short-sighted beasts — or else in their anger or alarm they will blindly charge the hunter, who then is forced to shoot to save himself from being tossed and gored on that great horn.   There was a hyena disturbing the other game, and as these are savage nuisances, Mr. Roosevelt shot this one at three hundred and fifty paces.   While the porters were taking the skin, he could not help laughing, he says, at finding their party in the center of a great plain, stared at from all sides by enough wild animals to stock a circus.   Vultures were flying overhead.   The three rhinoceros were gazing at them, about half a mile away.   Wildebeest (sometimes called gnu) which look something like the American buffalo or bison, and hartebeest, stood around in a ring, looking on.   Four or five antelope came in closer to see what was happening, and a zebra trotted by, neighing and startling the rhinoceros.

After a rest for luncheon, they went on, looking for lions.   Two wart-hogs jumped up, and Mr. Roosevelt shot the biggest of them.   By this time it was getting late in the afternoon; time for lions to be about.   At last they saw one; a big lioness. She ran along the bed of a stream, crouching so as not to be seen in the failing light.   The two

hunters rode past and would have missed her if
one of the native followers had not sighted her a
second time. Then Roosevelt and the other
hunter left their horses, and came in close on foot.
This is perhaps as dangerous as any hunting in
Africa. A man must be cool and a good shot to
go after lions; sooner or later almost every lion
hunter either gets badly hurt or gets killed.

This time all went well; Roosevelt hit her with
his first shot; ran in close and finished her. She
weighed over three hundred pounds. The porters
— much excited, as they always are at the death
of a lion — wished to carry the whole body without skinning it, back to camp. While they were
lashing it to a pole another lion began to growl
hungrily. The night was dark, without a moon,
and the work of getting back was hard for the
porters, as well as rather terrifying to them.
Lions were grunting all about; twice one of them
kept alongside the men as they walked,— much to
their discomfort. Then a rhinoceros, nearby, let
of a series of snorts, like a locomotive. This did
not cheer up the porters to any great degree.
Roosevelt and the other white hunter had trouble
to keep them together and to keep on the watch,
with their rifles ready to drive off any animals
which might attack.

At last they came to the camp of a tribe of sav-

ages called Masai.   As they were still four miles
from their own camp and as the porters were
about exhausted from carrying the lion, they decided to go in there, skin the lion and rest for a
while.   There was some trouble about this, as
the Masai feared that the scent of the dead lion
would scare their cattle.   They agreed at last,
however, admitted the white men and the porters,
and stood about, in the fire-light, leaning on their
spears, and laughing, while the lion was being
skinned.   They gave Roosevelt milk to drink and
seemed pleased to have a call from " Bwana
Makuba," the Great Chief, as the porters called
him.

So here was an Ex-President of the United
States, not many months from his work as Chief
Magistrate in the Capitol of a civilized nation,
talking to a group of savages, who in their
dwellings, weapons, clothing and customs had
hardly changed in three thousand years; the
twentieth century A. D. meeting the tenth century
B. C.

At ten o'clock they got back to their own camp,
and after a hot bath, sat down to a supper of eland
venison and broiled spurfowl,—" and surely no
supper ever tasted more delicious."

Another day, when hunting with the same companion he had the experience of being charged by

a wounded lion. It was a big, male lion, with a black and yellow mane. They chased him on horseback for about two miles. Then he stopped and hid behind a bush. A shot wounded him slightly and Mr. Tarlton, Roosevelt's companion, an experienced lion-hunter, told him that the lion was sure to charge.

Again I knelt and fired; but the mass of hair on the lion made me think he was nearer than he was, and I undershot, inflicting a flesh wound that was neither crippling nor fatal. He was already grunting savagely and tossing his tail erect, with his head held low; and at the shot the great sinewy beast came toward us with the speed of a greyhound. Tarlton then very properly fired, for lion hunting is no child's play, and it is not good to run risks. Ordinarily it is a very mean thing to experience joy at a friend's miss; but this was not an ordinary case, and I felt keen delight when the bullet from the badly sighted rifle missed, striking the ground many yards short. I was sighting carefully from my knee, and I knew I had the lion all right; for though he galloped at a great pace he came on steadily — ears laid back, and uttering terrific coughing grunts — and there was now no question of making allowance for distance, nor, as he was out in the open, for the fact that he had not before been distinctly visible. The bead of my fore-sight was exactly on the center of his chest as I pressed the trigger, and the bullet went as true as if the place had been plotted with dividers. The blow brought him up all standing, and he fell forward on his head.

The soft-nosed Winchester bullet had gone straight through the chest cavity, smashing the lungs and the big blood-vessels of the heart. Painfully he recovered his feet, and tried to come on, his ferocious courage holding out to the last; but he staggered and turned from side to side, unable to stand firmly, still less to advance at a faster pace than a walk. He had not ten seconds to live; but it is a sound principle to take no chances with lions. Tarlton hit him with his second bullet probably in the shoulder; and with my next shot I broke his neck. I had stopped him when he was still a hundred yards away, and certainly no finer sight could be imagined than that of this great maned lion as he charged.[1]

To the man who can shoot straight, and shoot just as straight at a savage animal as at a target, African game-hunting is for part of the time not very dangerous. Nine or ten lions or elephants or rhinoceros may be killed, without seeming risk. The tenth time something unexpected happens, and death comes very near to the hunter.

In shooting an elephant in the forest one day, Roosevelt had what was perhaps his closest call since the bear nearly killed him, years before in Idaho. He had just shot an elephant, when there came a surprise:

But at that very instant, before there was a moment's time in which to reload, the thick bushes parted im-

[1] "African Game Trails," pp. 192-3.

mediately on my left front, and through them surged
the vast bulk of a charging bull elephant, the matted
mass of tough creepers snapping like packthread before
his rush. He was so close that he could have touched
me with his trunk. I leaped to one side and dodged behind a tree trunk, opening the rifle, throwing out the
empty shells, and slipping in two cartridges. Meantime Cunninghame fired right and left, at the same time
throwing himself into the bushes on the other side.
Both his bullets went home, and the bull stopped short
in his charge, wheeled, and immediately disappeared in
the thick cover. We ran forward, but the forest had
closed over his wake. We heard him trumpet shrilly,
and then all sounds ceased.[1]

[1] "African Game Trails," p. 251.

CHAPTER XII

AT Khartoum Mr. Roosevelt and his son were joined by other members of his family. They all crossed to Europe, for he had been invited by the rulers and learned bodies of a number of countries to pay them a visit. He went to Italy, Austria, Germany, Norway, Sweden, Holland, France, Denmark, Belgium and England, receiving the highest compliments from their rulers, honorary degrees from the universities, and a welcome from the people everywhere which had been given with such heartiness to no other American since General Grant traveled round the world after the Civil War.

In Norway he spoke to the Nobel Committee in thanks for the Peace Prize which they had awarded him after the Russo-Japanese War. In Germany, the Kaiser ordered a review of troops for him; and he was received by the University of Berlin. In Paris, he addressed the famous institution of learning, the Sorbonne. The English universities received him, and gave him their honorary degrees. London made him a " freeman." His speeches before the learned men of Europe might not have been extraordinary for a university teacher, but when we think that his life had alternated between the hustle of politics, the career of a ranchman, of a soldier, and of a hunter of big game, it is evident that we shall have to search long and far among our public men before we can find any to match him in the variety of his interests and achievements.

In England, King Edward VII had just died, and Mr. Roosevelt was appointed by President Taft as the American representative at the funeral. There was a gathering in London of thirteen reigning monarchs, and many curious stories are told about the occasion. Of course the Kaiser was there, strutting about and trying to patronize everybody. Mr. Roosevelt had been politely received by the Kaiser and believed, as did every one, that beneath his arrogant manners, there was a great deal of ability. But he did not allow himself to be treated by the " All Highest " with magnificent condescension.

A story is repeated, of which one version is that the Kaiser suddenly called out, at some reception:

" Oh, Colonel Roosevelt, I wish to see you before I leave London, and can give you just thirty minutes, to-morrow afternoon at two."

" That's very good of Your Majesty," replied Mr. Roosevelt, " and I'll be there. But unfortunately I have an engagement, so that I'll only be able to give you twenty minutes."

Another story concerns a little boy,— the Crown Prince of one of the countries where royal folk have simpler and better manners than in Germany. He and his parents and other persons of royal rank were at the palace where Mr. Roosevelt was staying. As any man would know, boys are interested in much the same things whether they are princes or not, and this one was greatly taken by Mr. Roosevelt's stories of hunting, and by being taught some of the games which the American father and his boys had played in the White House, not many years before. So it happened that as a group of the visitors, including two or three kings and queens, stepped out of one of the rooms of the palace into a corridor one evening, they were astonished to see a gentleman down on his hands and knees on a rug, playing " bear " with a little boy. The gentleman was the Ex-President of the United States, and the boy was the future King of one of the countries of Europe.

Roosevelt's return to New York was the signal

PRESIDENT ROOSEVELT IN THE SADDLE

for a tremendous reception.   New York outdid
itself in salutes, parades, and wildly cheering
crowds.   Nothing like it had been seen before.
Even after the excitement of the first day of his
return, he could not go out without being surrounded by cheering crowds.   He knew that it
could not last, and said to his sister: " Soon they
will be throwing rotten apples at me."

He was right.   A period was about to begin
when he was to be defeated in every campaign
in which he engaged.   All the enemies he had
made in his long fight for better government —
and they were many and bitter enemies — were
to join hands with all the people who opposed him
just because they disliked him.   He was to part
company from some of his nearest friends, and
persistently to be reviled, misunderstood and attacked.   Yet he was to rally around him a body
of devoted friends, and make these the greatest
years of his life.

It is partly comic and partly sad, to look back
and consider the things for which Roosevelt had
fought in his public life, and to recall that a fight
had to be made for things like these; that the
man advocating them had to stand unlimited
abuse.   He had been abused for trying to stop
the sale of liquor to children, and opposed in his
efforts to prevent the making of cigars in filthy

bed-roooms.   He had been violently attacked for
enforcing the liquor laws of New York.   Lawyers and public men had grown red with anger
as they denounced him as a tyrant, and an enemy
to the Constitution, because he wished to stop
a dishonest system of rebates by the railroads.   A
man looks back and wonders if he were living
among sane people, or in a mad-house, when he re-
calls that Roosevelt was viciously attacked because
he proposed that the meat-packers of this country
should not be allowed to sell to their countrymen
rotten and diseased products which foreign countries refused even to admit.   Sneers greeted his
attempts to prevent poisons being sold as medicine, and laudanum being peddled to little children
as soothing-syrup.   His fight to prevent greedy
folk from destroying the forests, wasting the
minerals, and spoiling the water supplies of
America had to be made in the face of every sort
of legal trickery and the meanest of personal
abuse.

The Republican Party had been founded during one of the greatest efforts for human free-
dom ever made in our history.   In its long years
in power, and in the amazing increase in prosperity and wealth in America, it had become the
defender of wealth.   Many of its highest and
most powerful men could see no farther than the

cash drawer.   Human rights and wrongs, human suffering, or any attempt to prevent such sufferings, simply did not interest them.   They were not cruel men personally, but they had heard repeated for so many years that this or the other thing could not be done " because it would hurt business," that they had come to worship " business " as a savage bows his head before an idol. Many of them could give money for an orphan asylum or a children's hospital, and yet on the same day, vote to kill a bill aimed to prevent child-labor.   To pass such a bill as that would " hurt business."

The Democratic Party was no better.   It was simply weaker, and usually less intelligent. Wherever it was powerful, it, too, was apt to be the servant of corruption.   The politicians of both parties loved to keep up a continual fight about the tariff, to distract public attention from other important subjects.

There had been disagreements in the Republican Party for a number of years.   These had gone on during the Roosevelt administration. In the main, these struggles can be described by saying that President Roosevelt and those who agreed with him were looking out for the advantage of the many, and for the welfare and health of great masses of the people.   His opponents

were more interested to see that nothing checked
the activities of great corporations, railroads, and
manufacturing interests.   They sincerely believed
that this was the first concern of all true patriots.
Roosevelt wished every man to have a square
deal, an equal chance, so far as possible, to earn
as good a living as he could.   His opponents
thought that if the great business interests could
only go on, as they liked, without being annoyed
by the government, they would be able to give
employment to almost everybody, and to all the
unfortunates, who were crushed in the struggle,
they would give charity.

Between these two groups there was a cease-
less fight all the years Roosevelt was in the White
House.   He had been strongly approved at the
polls; many of the measures he advocated had been
made laws by Congress.   So he thought, and the
larger part of the Republican Party thought, when
Mr. Taft became President, that the measures
which they had approved were going to be ad-
vanced still further.

It soon appeared that they were in for a dis-
appointment.   Mr. Taft proved friendly to the
older politicians; the younger and progressive
men were not in favor.   He made his associates,
and chose as his advisers, the men who called

Mr. Roosevelt " rash," " a socialist," " an anarchist." Many of the men who surrounded
President Taft were honest and patriotic. But
there were also a number of stick-in-the-mud
statesmen,— old gentlemen who had been saying the same thing, thinking the same things,
doing the same things, for forty years. To
change, to be up with the times, to progress, to
alter methods to meet new conditions, struck
them as simply indecent. Their idea of a
happy national life was great " prosperity " for
a fortunate few, a lesser degree of success
for some others who could cling to the chariot
wheels of the rich, and,— charity for the rest.
That was always their answer to the old, hard
problem of wealth and poverty. Like quack
doctors they would try to cure the symp-
toms, rather than like wise physicians seek to
find the causes. They were like the Tories in
our Revolution who were for King George
against George Washington, because King George
was the legal King of the American colonies, or
like the Northern pro-slavery men, who defended
slavery because it was permitted by the Constitution and the slaves were legal " property." The
Constitution was, for them, an instrument to be
used to block all change, whether good or bad.

Other men, near to President Taft, were neither patriotic nor innocent. They were shrewd, powerful Bosses,— men of the type of Platt. Only, Mr. Taft did not stand on the alert with them, as Roosevelt had done as Governor, working with them when he could, and fighting them when they went wrong. He allowed them to influence his administration, and, at last, accepted a nomination engineered by them for their own selfish purposes.

The Republicans who followed President Taft, the "stand-patters," believed in property rights first, and human rights second. If any of them did not actually believe this, they joined people who did thoroughly believe it, and so their action counted toward putting that belief into practice. The others, the "Insurgents" or Progressive Republicans, (later called the Bull Moose) believed in human rights first. That is as near as the thing can be stated, remembering that it was a disputed point, with good men on both sides. The stand-patters said the Progressives were cranks,— visionary and impractical; the Progressives replied that it was better to be both of these things than to be quite so near to the earth and selfish as Mr. Taft's followers or managers. The events of later years have not borne out the contention that Roosevelt was "rash" and "dan-

gerous "; while the charge that Mr. Taft made a
President more pleasing to the Bosses than to the
people was amply proved, in the campaign of
1912.

CHAPTER XIII

THE BULL MOOSE

IT was not personal ambition which made Roosevelt become the leader of the revolt in the Republican Party, and later head a new party. The revolt had been growing while he was in Africa, and he was long besought to become its leader. At first, Senator La Follette seemed a possible leader, but he broke down in a nervous attack, and the belief that he was not the man for the place has been justified by later events.

As President Taft's administration drew to an end, in 1911 and 1912, it was clear that he was steadily losing the public confidence. State elections, and other straws, showed how the wind was blowing. The Progressive Republicans pointed out to their fellow-members of the party that only where a Progressive ran for office in a state election did the party win. Otherwise the Democrats were victorious. The lesson was plain; but the stand-patters did not care to see it. By the beginning of 1912 it was freely predicted in print that the Democrats would nominate

Governor Wilson of New Jersey, their strongest
candidate, and that they would win if the Republicans insisted on naming Mr. Taft. But the
old-line Republicans were above taking advice.
The Democrats were naturally gleeful about the
situation; they kept their faces straight and solemnly warned the Republicans, in the name of the
safety of the country, not to listen to the " wild
man," Roosevelt, but to be sure to nominate Mr.
Taft. And the Republicans listened to the advice
of their opponents. " Whom the Gods would destroy they first make mad."

Roosevelt had been telling his friends that he
would not run again; that he did not wish to oppose Mr. Taft, who had been his close friend and
associate. But neither he, nor the Republicans
who thought as he did, liked to see their party
drift back and back to become the organization
for plunder which the Bosses would have made it
long before, if they had always had a " good-
natured " man in the White House. When the
governors of seven States — Michigan, West Vir-
ginia, Wyoming, Nebraska, New Hampshire,
Missouri and Kansas — united in an appeal to
Roosevelt for leadership, he began to change his
mind.

He said in private, that he knew it would be
hard, if not impossible, for him to get the nom-

ination; President Taft had all the machinery on his side. He knew that it meant parting with many of his best friends; the older politicians would mainly oppose him; he would have to go directly to the people for his support, and rely upon the younger leaders as his lieutenants.

In going straight to the people he was following one of the principles of the Insurgent or Progressive Republicans. In order to fight the Bosses, and overcome the crooked and secret influence of "big business" in politics. the Progressives were proposing various methods by which it was hoped the people might rule more directly, and prevent a few men from overcoming the wishes of the many. One of these methods was the direct primary, so that the voters might choose their candidates themselves, instead of leaving it to the absurd conventions, where large crowds of men are hired to fill the galleries, yell for one candidate, and try to out-yell the opposing crowd.

In February, 1912, Roosevelt announced that he was a candidate for the Republican nomination.

" My hat is in the ring," he said.

The storm of abuse which raged around him now was terrific. All the friends of fattened monopoly — and this included many of the most powerful newspapers — screamed aloud in their fright. Mostly they assailed him on three counts:

that he was " disloyal " to his friend, Mr. Taft,
that he had promised never to run for President
again; and that it meant the overthrow of the Republic and the setting up of a monarchy if any
man ever disregarded Washington's example and
was President for three terms.

The charge of disloyalty to Mr. Taft does not
deserve discussion. Those who made it never
stopped to think that they were saying that a
man should set his personal friendships higher
than his regard for the nation; that he must support his friend, even if he believed that to do so
would work harm to the whole country. Moreover, if there had been any disloyalty, it had not
been on Mr. Roosevelt's side! He had remained
true to his principles. As for the promise never
to run again, we have already seen what he said
about that. The notion that Washington laid
down some law against reëlecting a President for
more than two terms is an example of how a
complete error may pass into popular belief. and
become a superstition. Washington said and believed the very opposite. He did not wish a third
term himself, because he was old and weary, but
in regard to third terms he seems to have been
even more liberal than Roosevelt, who disapproved
of three terms *in succession*. But Washington
distinctly said that he saw no reason why a Presi-

dent should not be reëlected as often as the people needed his services.   He said nothing about four, eight, or twelve years, but in discussing this very question in a letter to Lafayette, wrote:

" I can see no propriety in precluding ourselves from the services of any man, who on some emergency shall be deemed most capable of serving the public." [1]

In the primary campaign, in the spring of 1912, the Progressive Republicans and Mr. Roosevelt proved their case up to the hilt.   In every instance but one, where it was possible to get a direct vote of the people, Roosevelt beat President Taft, and overwhelmingly.   Thus, in California he beat him nearly two to one; in Illinois, more than two to one, in Nebraska more than three to one, in North Dakota more than twenty to one, in South Dakota more than three to one.   In New Jersey, Maryland, Oregon and Ohio, Roosevelt won decisively; in Pennsylvania by a tremendous majority. Massachusetts, the only remaining State which held a direct primary, where both men were in the field, split nearly even, giving Mr. Taft a small lead.

In the face of this clear indication of what the voters wished, for the Republican leaders to go

[1] Sparks, " Writings of George Washington," ix. 358.

ahead and nominate Mr. Taft was sheer suicide
from a political point of view.   It was also something much worse: the few denying the will of
the many.   This, of course, is tyranny,— what
our ancestors revolted against when they founded
the nation.   But go ahead they did.   It is prob-
able that even as early as this they had no idea of
winning the election; they merely intended to keep
the party machinery in their own hands.   Gravely
talking about law and the Constitution they pro-
ceeded to defy the first principles of popular government.

By use of the Southern delegates, from States
where the Republican Party exists mostly in
theory, by contesting almost every delegation, and
always ruling against Roosevelt, by every manipu-
lation which the " Old Guard " of the party could
employ, Mr. Taft was nominated.   In at least
one important and crucial case, delegates were
seized for Mr. Taft by shameless theft.   The
phrase is that used by Mr. Thayer,— a historian,
accustomed to weigh his words, and a non-parti-
san in this contest, since he favored neither Mr.
Taft nor Roosevelt.

In August the Progressive Party was founded
at a convention held in Chicago.   Roosevelt and
Johnson were the nominees for President and
Vice-President.   The men gathered at this con-

vention were out of the Republican Party; they
had not left it, but the party had left them.   Not
willingly did they take this action; men whose
grandfathers voted for Frémont in 1856 and for
Lincoln in 1860, and again for Lincoln in 1864,
when the fate of the Republic really depended on
the success of the Republican Party.   The sons of
men who had fought for the Union did not lightly
attack even the name of the old party.   But there
was nothing left but its name; its worst elements
led it; many of the better men who stayed in it
kept silent.   Probably even they realized the
nauseous hypocrisy of the situation when Mr.
William Barnes of New York came forward and
implored that the country be saved, that our liberty
be saved, that the Constitution be saved!

For the destroyer, from whom the country was
to be saved, was one of the greatest and most
honorable men of his time,— while it was later
established in court that it was no libel to say
that Mr. Barnes was a Boss and had used crooked
methods.

The Progressives, soon called the Bull Moose
Party, attracted the usual group of reformers,
and some cranks.   Each new party does this.
Roosevelt had, many years before, spoken of the
"lunatic fringe" which clings to the skirts of
every sincere reform.

" But the whole body," writes Mr. Thayer, " judged without prejudice, probably contained the largest number of disinterested, public-spirited, and devoted persons, who had ever met for a national and political object since the group which formed the Republican Party in 1854."

All the new measures which they proposed, although denounced by the two old parties, were in use in other democratic countries; many of them have since been adopted here. Roosevelt foresaw the radical wave which was later to sweep over the country and was trying to make our government more liberal, so as to meet the new spirit of things. The more radical of Socialists always hated him as their worst enemy, for they knew that his reasonable reforms would make it impossible for them to succeed in their extreme proposals.

The jokes made about the new party were often most amusing and added a great deal of interest to an exciting campaign. The Bull Moosers were very much in earnest, and had a camp-meeting fervor, which laid them open to a good deal of ridicule. But they could stand it, for they knew that as between themselves and the Republicans. the last laugh would be theirs. The Republicans had nominated Mr. Taft by means of delegates from rock-ribbed Democratic States like Alabama,

Florida and Georgia, let them now see if they could elect him by such means!

One phase of the campaign was a shame and a disgrace. The Republican newspapers joined in the use of abusive terms against Roosevelt, to a degree which has never been paralleled, before nor since. They described him as a monster, a foul traitor, another Benedict Arnold, and for weeks used language about him for which the writers would be overcome with shame if it were brought home to them now. This had its natural result. Just as the speeches of Emma Goldman and others stirred up the murderer of President McKinley to his act, so this reiteration of abuse, this harping on the assertion that Roosevelt was the enemy of the country, the destroyer of law and liberty, induced another weak-minded creature to attempt murder.

A man named Schrank who said that he had been led on by what he read in the papers, waited for Roosevelt outside a hotel in Milwaukee. This was during the campaign and Roosevelt was leaving the hotel to make a speech in a public hall. As he stood up in his automobile, Schrank shot him in the chest. The bullet was partially checked by a thick roll of paper — the notes for his speech — and by an eye-glasses case. Never-

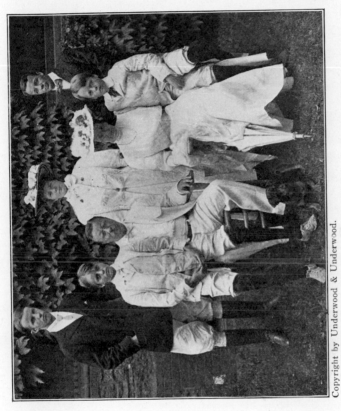

PRESIDENT AND MRS. ROOSEVELT WITH FIVE OF THEIR CHILDREN

theless, with the bullet in him, only stopping to change his blood-soaked shirt, he refused to quit. He went and made his speech, standing on the platform and speaking for over an hour.

He thought of himself as a soldier fighting for a cause, and he would no more leave because of a wound than he would have deserted his fellow-hunter in Africa, when that charging lion came down on them.

For two weeks he had to keep out of the campaign, recovering from his wound, first in a hospital and then at home. Governor Wilson, the Democratic nominee, soon to be the President-Elect, generously offered to cease his campaign speeches, but this offer was declined by Mr. Roosevelt.

In the election, Mr. Wilson was the winner, with Mr. Roosevelt second. The Progressive candidate beat the Republican, as it had been predicted he would. Mr. Roosevelt received over half a million more votes than Mr. Taft, and had eighty-eight electoral votes to eight for Mr. Taft. The Bosses were punished for defying the will of the voters and a useful lesson in politics was administered.

The testimony of Mr. Thayer is especially valuable, since he was a supporter of Mr. Wilson in

this election.   He writes that since the election
showed that Roosevelt had been all the time the
real choice of the Republican Party " it was the
Taft faction and not Roosevelt which split the
Republican Party in 1912."

CHAPTER XIV

THE EXPLORER

I cannot rest from travel; I will drink
Life to the lees. All times I have enjoy'd
Greatly, have suffered greatly, both with those
That loved me, and alone; on shore, and when
Thro' scudding drifts the rainy Hyades
Vext the dim sea. I am become a name;
For always roaming with a hungry heart
Much have I seen and known,— cities of men
And manners, climates, councils, governments,
Myself not least, but honor'd of them all,—
And drunk delight of battle with my peers,
Far on the ringing plains of windy Troy. . . .
How dull it is to pause, to make an end,
To rust unburnish'd, not to shine in use!
As tho' to breathe were life! Life piled on life
Were all too little, and of one to me
Little remains; but every hour is saved
From that eternal silence, something more,
A bringer of new things; and vile it were
For some three suns to store and hoard myself,
And this grey spirit yearning in desire
To follow knowledge like a sinking star,
Beyond the utmost bound of human thought.
                    TENNYSON'S *Ulysses*.

MR. ROOSEVELT took his defeat without whimpering. When he was in a fight he gave blows and expected to receive them. His enemies often hit foul blows, and this his friends resented, especially when the attacks actually provoked an attempt at murder. When his private character was assailed he defended himself, promptly and successfully. But neither he nor any of his friends asked that he should be sacred from all criticism; nor feebly protested that he was above ordinary mortals, and only to be mentioned with a sort of trembling reverence. He was too much of a man to be kept wrapped in wool.

In 1913 he traveled through South American countries to speak before learned bodies which had invited him to come before them. Afterwards, with his son Kermit, some American naturalists, and Colonel Rondon, a brave and distinguished Brazilian officer, he made a long trip through the wilderness of Brazil, to hunt and explore. Some of the country through which they traveled was little known to white men; some of it absolutely unknown. They hunted and killed specimens of the jaguar, tapir, peccary, and nearly all of the other strange South American animals.

In February 1914, they set out upon an unknown stream called the River of Doubt. They did not know whether the exploration of this river would take them weeks or months; whether they might have to face starvation, or savage tribes, or worse than either, disease. They surveyed the river as they went, so as to be able to map its course, and add to geographical knowledge. Strange birds haunted the river, and vicious stinging insects annoyed the travelers. They constantly had to carry the canoes around rapids or waterfalls, so that progress was slow. Some of the canoes were damaged and others had to be built. Large birds, like the curassow, and also monkeys, were shot for food. The pest of stinging insects grew constantly worse,— bees, mosquitoes, large blood-sucking flies and enormous ants tormented them. The flies were called piums and borashudas. Some of them bit like scorpions.

Kermit Roosevelt's canoe was caught in the rapids, smashed and sunk, and one of the men drowned. Once they saw signs of some unknown tribe of Indians, when one of the dogs belonging to the party was killed in the forest, almost within sight of Colonel Rondon, and found with two arrows in his body. The river was dangerous for bathing, because of a peculiar fish — the piranha — a savage little beast which attacks men and animals with its razor-like teeth, inflicts fearful wounds and may even kill any unfortunate creature which is caught by a school in deep water. Some members of the party were badly bitten by the piranhas.

As their long and difficult course down the river

continued, and as their hardships increased, one of the native helpers murdered another native — a sergeant — and fled. Roosevelt, while in the water helping to right an upset canoe, bruised his leg against a boulder. Inflammation set in, as it usually does with wounds in the tropics. For forty-eight days they saw no human being outside their own party. They were all weak with fever and troubled with wounds received in the river. Colonel Roosevelt (who was nearly fifty· six years old) wrote of his own condition:

The after effects of the fever still hung on; and the leg which had been hurt while working in the rapids with the sunken canoe had taken a turn for the bad and developed an abscess. The good doctor, to whose unwearied care and kindness I owe much, had cut it open and inserted a drainage tube; an added charm being given the operation, and the subsequent dressings, by the enthusiasm with which the piums and boroshudas took part therein. I could hardly hobble, and was pretty well laid up. " But " there aren't no ' stop con- ductor,' while a battery's changing ground." No man has any business to go on such a trip as ours unless he will refuse to jeopardize the welfare of his associates by any delay caused by a weakness or ailment of his. It is his duty to go forward, if necessary on all fours, until he drops. Fortunately, I was put to no such test. I remained in good shape until we had passed the last of the rapids of the chasms. When my serious trouble came we had only canoe-riding ahead of us. It is not ideal for a sick man to spend the hottest hours of the day stretched on the boxes in the bottom of a small open dugout, under the well-nigh intolerable heat of the torrid sun of the mid-tropics, varied by blinding, drenching downpours of rain; but I could not be sufficiently grateful for the chance. Kermit and Cherrie took care of me as if they had been trained nurses; and Colonel Rondon and Lyra were no less thoughtful.[1]

It is known that his illness was more serious, and his conduct much more unselfish than he told in his book. When he could not be moved, he asked the others to go forward for their own safety and leave him. They refused, naturally, and he secretly resolved to shoot himself if his condition did not soon improve, rather than be a drag on the party.

In his report to the Brazilian Government, which had made the expedition possible by its aid, Mr. Roosevelt was able to say:

"We have put on the map a river about 1500 kilometers in length running from just south of the 13th degree to north of the 5th degree and the biggest affluent of the Madeira. Until now its upper course has been utterly unknown to every one, and its lower course, although known for years to the rubber men, utterly unknown to cartographers."

[1] "Through the Brazilian Wilderness," p. 319.

The Brazilian Government renamed the river in his honor, first the Rio Roosevelt, later the Rio Téodoro. Branches of it were named in honor of other members of the party, the Rio Kermit and the Rio Cherrie,— the latter for the American naturalist, Mr. George K. Cherrie.

CHAPTER XV

THE MAN

WHAT did Theodore Roosevelt do during his life that raised him above other men? What were his achievements? Why are memorials and monuments raised in his honor, books written about him? Why do people visit his grave, and care to preserve the house where he was born?

First, because he helped the cause of better government all his life, as, while in college, he said that he was going to do.

Second, because he had a good influence on politics, upon business, and upon American life generally. Dishonest and shady dealings which were common when he left college, became very much less common as a result of his work. No other American did as much as he for this improvement.

Third, because he practiced the " square deal." It did not matter to him if the evil-doer was rich or poor,— Roosevelt was his enemy. The criminal who had many friends in Wall Street was a criminal still in his eyes; and the rascal who had friends in labor unions was nevertheless a rascal to him. He would not denounce one and go easy with the other. Poisoning people with bad meat was no less a crime to him because it was said to be done in the interests of " business "; blowing up people with bombs was not to be considered any less than murder because some one said it was done to help " labor."

Next, he practiced what he preached. When the great time came, he was ready " to pay with his body for his soul's desire."

While President, he proved by his conduct of our relations with foreign countries, that it is possible both to keep peace and to keep our self respect, and that this can be done only by firmness and courage.

He maintained our national defenses at the highest possible level, scorning to risk his fellow-countrymen's lives and fortunes through neglect of the Army and Navy.

By his wisdom, promptness and moral courage in an emergency he made the Panama Canal possible.

He led in a great fight for liberal politics, trying to put the ruling power of the nation once more in the hands of its citizens, and showing by his action that his country was dearer to him than any political party.

Finally, in the very last years of his life, and in a time of dreadful national trial, his great voice became the true voice of America to lead his countrymen out of a quagmire of doubt and disloyalty.

You may have heard it said that he was conceited, arrogant, head-strong. What did the men nearest him think? John Hay, the polished diplomat, who had been private secretary to Abraham Lincoln, wrote about Roosevelt in his diary. November 28, 1904:

I read the President's message in the afternoon. . . . Made several suggestions as to changes and omissions. The President came in just as I had finished and we went over the matter together. He accepted my ideas with that singular amiability and open-mindedness which form so striking a contrast with the general idea of his brusque and arbitrary character.

You may have heard it said that he acted hastily, went ahead on snap-judgments. On this subject, Mr. Hay wrote:

Roosevelt is prompt and energetic, but he takes infinite pains to get at the facts before he acts. In all the crises in which he has been accused of undue haste, his action has been the result of long meditation and well-reasoned conviction. If he thinks rapidly, that is no fault; he thinks thoroughly, and that is the essential.

He was never a humbug.   He did not deny that
he enjoyed being President.   He never let his
friends point to him, while he was in the White
House, as a martyr.   He had a good time wherever he was.   As he wrote:

I remember once sitting at a table with six or eight
other public officials, and each was explaining how he
regarded being in public life — how only the sternest
sense of duty prevented him from resigning his office,
and how the strain of working for a thankless con-
stituency was telling upon him — and that nothing but
the fact that he felt that he ought to sacrifice his com-
fort to the welfare of his country kept him in the
arduous life of statesmanship.   It went round the table
until it came to my turn.   This was during my first
term of office as President of the United States.   I said:
" Now, gentlemen, I do not wish there to be any mis-
understanding.   I like my job, and I want to keep it for
four years more." [1]

As for the question whether he acted from personal ambition, or from devotion to the cause he
represented, the following incident is as strong a
piece of evidence as we have about any of our public men.   It is related by Mr. Travers Carman,
of the *Outlook,* who accompanied Colonel Roosevelt to the Republican convention in 1912.

Roosevelt, on the evening of this conference in
the Congress Hotel, lacked only twenty-eight

[1] Abbott, p. 100.

votes to secure the nomination for President. Mr. Carman was in the room, when a delegate entered, in suppressed excitement, announcing that he represented thirty-two Southern delegates who would pledge themselves to vote for the Colonel, if they could be permitted to vote with the " regular " Republicans on all matters of party organization, upon the platform, and so on. Here were thirty-two votes,— four more than were needed to give him the nomination.

Without a moment's hesitation and in the death-like silence of that room the Colonel's answer rang out, clearly and distinctly : " Thank the delegates you represent, but tell them that I cannot permit them to vote for me unless they vote for all progressive principles for which I have fought, for which the Progressive element in the Republican party stands, and by which I stand or fall." Strong men broke down under the stress of that night. Life-long friends of Mr. Roosevelt endeavored to persuade him to reconsider his decision. After listening patiently he turned to two who had been urging him to accept the offer of the Southern delegates, placed a hand on the shoulder of each, and said: " I have grown to regard you both as brothers; let no act or word of yours make that relationship impossible." [1]

Two important law-suits occupied some of Roosevelt's time after the Progressive campaign.

[1] Abbott, p. 85.

One of the favorite slanders about Roosevelt, repeated mostly by word of mouth, was that he drank to excess or was an habitual drunkard. At last it began to be repeated in print; a Michigan newspaper printed it, coupled with other falsehoods concerning his use of profane language. Few public men would have cared to bring suit, because the plaintiff must stand a cross-examination. But Roosevelt was careful of his good name; he did not intend that persons should be able to repeat slander about him, except in deliberate bad faith.

He and his lawyers went to the trial, bringing with them dozens of witnesses. life-long friends, hunting companions, reporters who had accompanied him on political campaigns. fellow-soldiers, Cabinet officers, physicians, officers of the Army and Navy. These witnesses testified for a week to his temperate habits, agreeing absolutely in their testimony. The doctors pointed out that only a temperate man could have recovered so quickly from his wound. It was established that he never drank anything stronger than wine, except as a medicine; that he drank very little wine, and never got drunk.

At the end, the newspaper editor withdrew his statement, apologized, was found guilty and fined only nominal charges. Mr. Roosevelt was not after this small creature's money, but was only bent on clearing his reputation. So it was at his request that the fine was fixed at six cents.

Mr. William Barnes, the Albany politician, sued Mr. Roosevelt for libel, because Roosevelt had called him a Boss, and said that he used crooked methods. This had been said in a political campaign. The Republicans were looking for some chance to destroy Roosevelt, and Mr. Barnes, aided by an able Republican lawyer, thought that they would be doing a great service if they could besmirch Mr. Roosevelt in some way.

So they worked their hardest and best, cross-examined him for days and searched every incident of his political life. At the end they joined that large band of disappointed men who tried to destroy Roosevelt or catch him in something disreputable. For the jury decided in Mr. Roosevelt's favor, indicating that he had uttered no untruth when he made his remarks about Mr. Barnes.

As a writer, Mr. Roosevelt would have made a name for himself, if he had done nothing else. The success of his books is not due to the high offices which he held, for his best writings had nothing to do with politics. As a writer on politics he was forceful and clear. There was no doubt as to the meaning of his state papers; they

never had to be explained nor " interpreted."
They were not designed to mean any one of two
or three things, according to later circumstances.
Strength and directness were the characteristics.
When writing about the by-ways of politics his
enjoyment of the ridiculous made his work especially readable.   When he felt deeply about any
great issue, as in his last years, about the Great
War, and our part in it, his indignation found
its way into his pages, which became touched with
the fire of genuine eloquence.

He wrote about books and animals, and about
outdoor life, as no President has ever done.   His
remarks upon literature are those of a great book-
lover, sensible, well-informed and free from pose.

Every one should read his " Autobiography,"
his " Hero Tales from American History " which
he wrote in company with Senator Lodge, and his
" Letters to His Children."   His early accounts
of hunting in the West make good reading, but in
his book about his African hunt, and in the one
on the South American trip, he probably reached
his highest level as a writer.   If any American
has written better books of travel than these,
more continuously interesting, fuller of pleasing
detail about the little incidents, the birds and tiny
animals which he encountered, and at the same
time with a stricter regard for accuracy of obser-

PRESIDENT THEODORE ROOSEVELT

vation, I do not know where they are to be found.

This man of politics had a true poetic feeling for the countries he visited; time and again he moves his readers in describing the wonders of the great waste places, the melancholy deserts and wildernesses, the deadly fascination of the jungle, and the awful glory of the tropic dawns and sunsets. When something awakened his imagination he could write passages full of the magic of poetry. Witness this, it is not a description of scenery, but a vision of the true historian of the future:

The true historian will bring the past before our eyes as if it were the present. He will make us see as living men the hard-faced archers of Agincourt, and the war-worn spear-men who followed Alexander down beyond the rim of the known world. We shall hear grate on the coast of Britain the keels of the Low-Dutch sea-thieves whose children's children were to inherit unknown continents. . . . Beyond the dim centuries we shall see the banners float above armed hosts. . . Dead poets shall sing to us of the deeds of men of might and the love and beauty of women. We shall see the dancing girls of Memphis. The scent of the flowers in the hanging gardens of Babylon will be heavy to our senses. We shall sit at feast with the kings of Nineveh when they drink from ivory and gold. . . . For us the war-horns of King Olaf shall wail across the flood, and the harps sound high at festivals in forgotten halls. The frowning strongholds of the barons of old shall rise before us, and the white palace-castles from whose windows Syrian princes once looked across the blue Ægean. . . . We shall see the terrible horsemen of Timur the Lame ride over the roof of the world; we shall hear the drums beat as the armies of Gustavus and Frederick and Napoleon drive forward to victory.[1]

Here is one of Mr. Roosevelt's anecdotes of an incident in the White House. It shows why the people were interested in that house while he lived in it:

" No guests were ever more welcome at the White House than these old friends of the cattle ranches and the cow camps — the men with whom I had ridden the long circle and eaten at the tail-board of a chuck-wagon — whenever they turned up at Washington during my Presidency. I remember one of them who appeared at Washington one day just before lunch, a huge powerful man, who, when I knew him, had been distinctly a fighting character. It happened that on that day another old friend, the British Ambassador, Mr. Bryce, was among those coming to lunch. Just before we went in I turned to my cow-puncher friend and said to him with great solemnity, ' Remember, Jim, that if you shot at the feet of the British Ambassador to make him dance, it would be likely to cause international complications '; to

[1] "History as Literature," p. 32, et seq.

which Jim responded with unaffected horror, 'Why, Colonel, I shouldn't think of it! I shouldn't think of it!'"[1]

And here is one about his children:

"The small boy was convalescing, and was engaged in playing on the floor with some tin ships, together with two or three pasteboard monitors and rams of my own manufacture. He was giving a vivid rendering of Farragut at Mobile Bay, from memories of how I had told the story. My pasteboard rams were fascinating — if a naval architect may be allowed to praise his own work — and as property they were equally divided between the little girl and the small boy. The little girl looked on with alert suspicion from the bed, for she was not yet convalescent enough to be allowed down on the floor. The small boy was busily reciting the phases of the fight, which now approached its climax, and the little girl evidently suspected that her monitor was destined to play the part of victim.

"Little boy. 'And then they steamed bang into the monitor.'

"Little girl. 'Brother, don't you sink my monitor!'

"Little boy (without heeding and hurrying

[1] "Autobiography," p. 132.

toward the climax). ' And the torpedo went at the monitor!'

" Little girl. ' My monitor is not to sink!'

" Little boy, dramatically; ' And bang the monitor sank!'

" Little girl. ' It didn't do any such thing. My monitor always goes to bed at seven, and it's now quarter past. My monitor was in bed and couldn't sink!' " [1]

[1] "Autobiography," p. 367.

CHAPTER XVI

THE GREAT AMERICAN

Death closes all; but something ere the end,
Some work of noble note, may yet be done. . . .
Tho' much is taken, much abides; and tho'
We are not now that strength which in old days
Moved earth and heaven, that which we are, we are,—
One equal temper of heroic hearts,
Made weak by time and fate, but strong in will
To strive, to seek, to find and not to yield.

TENNYSON'S *Ulysses.*

NOT many months after Roosevelt came back from South America, the Great War in Europe broke out. It is but dreaming now to surmise what might have been done in those fearful days of July 1914, when the German hordes were gathering for their attack upon the world. Once before, and singlehanded, this country had made the German Kaiser halt. Had there been resolution in the White House in 1914, could all the neutral nations have been rallied at our side, and could we have spoken in tones so decisive to the Hun that he would have drawn back even then, have left Belgium unravaged, and spared the world the misery of the next four years? It may be so;

Germany did not expect to have to take on England as an enemy. If she had been told, *so that there was no mistaking our meaning,* that she would have us against her as well, then it might have been her part to hesitate, and finally put back her sword.

Roosevelt supported the President at first, in his policy of neutrality, supposing him to have some special information. He supported him with hesitation, and with qualifications however, pointing out that neutrality is no proud position, and has many disadvantages. Perhaps he had some inklings of the danger to the country when our foreign affairs are managed by pacifists. Certainly America had noticed the grim fact that a Government which forever talked about peace had in actual practice, shed more blood in a few hours at Vera Cruz than had been spilled in all the seven years while Roosevelt was President. Moreover, this blood was shed uselessly; no object whatever having been gained by it.

It is impossible to understand Roosevelt; it is impossible to get any idea of what he did during his term of office; it is impossible to learn anything from his career, unless we contrast him and his beliefs and actions with the conduct of our Government during the Great War. An object lesson of the most illuminating sort is afforded by

this contrast, and we may make up our minds
about the wisest paths to be followed in the
future if we notice what Roosevelt said and did
at this time, how far and how wisely his counsel
was accepted or rejected.

He disapproved, for instance, President Wilson's speech, made a day or two after the sinking
of the *Lusitania* in which the President spoke of a
nation being "too proud to fight." Roosevelt
said that a nation which announced itself as too
proud to fight was usually about proud enough to
be kicked; and it must be admitted that the Germans took that view of it, and for a year and more
continued to kick. He did not deem it wise,
when President Wilson informed the Germans, ten
days later, that we remembered the "humane
attitude" of their Government "in matters of international right," for he happened to recall that
Belgium was at that moment red with the blood
of its citizens, slain by the Germans in a sort
of warfare that combined highway robbery
with revolting murder. Neither did it seem
useful to him to speak about German influence
as always "upon the side of justice and hu-
manity."

Mr. Roosevelt had always been strong for having the nation ready for war if war should come.
Mr. Wilson first said that persons who believed

this were nervous and excited. Next he joined
these persons himself, so far as words went, and
finally he let the matter drop until we were at
war. Mr. Roosevelt believed that when you once
were at war it was a crime to " hit softly."   Mr.
Wilson waited until we had been at war a year and
over, and then announced in a speech that he was
determined to use force!

Mr. Roosevelt wrote regularly for *The Outlook,* later for the *Metropolitan Magazine* and the
Kansas City Star.   Thousands of his countrymen
read his articles, and found in them the only expression of the American spirit which was being
uttered. Americans were puzzled, troubled and
finally humiliated by the letters and speeches
which came from Washington. To be told that
in this struggle between the blood-guilty Hun,
and the civilized nations of the earth, that we
must keep even our minds impartial seemed an
impossible command. School-boys throughout
the country must have wondered why President
Wilson, with every means for getting information, should have to confess that he did not
know what the war was about! And when Mr.
Wilson declared in favor of a peace without
victory, his friends and admirers were kept busy
explaining, some of them, that he meant without
victory for the Allies, and others that he meant

without victory for Germany, and still others that he meant without victory for anybody in particular.

No wonder that Americans began to wonder what country they were living in, and whether they had been mistaken in thinking that America had a heroic history, in which its citizens took pride. No wonder they turned their eyes to Europe, where scores of young Americans, sickening at the state of things at home, had eagerly volunteered to fight with France or England against the Hun. One of these, named Alan Seeger, who wrote the fine poem " I have a Rendezvous with Death," died in battle on our Independence Day. He also wrote a poem called " A Message to America." [1] In it he said that America had once a leader:

> . . . the man
> Most fit to be called American.

In it he spoke further of the same leader

> I have been too long from my country's shores
> To reckon what state of mind is yours,
> But as for myself I know right well
> I would go through fire and shot and shell
> And face new perils and make my bed
> In new privations, if *Roosevelt* led.

[1] Seeger.   Poems, pp. 164, 165.

One did not have to be long with the men who volunteered at the beginning of the war to know that Roosevelt's spirit led these men, and that they looked to him and trusted him as the great American. The country's honor was safe in his hands, and no mawkish nor cowardly words ever came from his lips.

He pointed out the folly of the pacifist type of public men, like Mr. Bryan and Mr. Ford. The latter, helpless as a butterfly in those iron years, led his quarreling group of pilgrims to Europe, on his " Peace Ship," and then left them to their incessant fights with each other. The American public was quick to see the contrast, when war came, and Roosevelt's four sons and son-in-law all volunteered, while Mr. Ford's son took advantage of some law and avoided military duty, in order to add more millions to his already enormous heap. The lesson of Roosevelt's teaching and example was not lost, and the people recognized that the country would endure while it had men like the Roosevelts, but that it would go down in infamy if the other sort became numerous.

In the election of 1916 Mr. Roosevelt, after refusing the Progressive nomination, supported Mr. Hughes, the Republican, against President Wilson. He tried hard to get Mr. Hughes to come out with some utterance which would put him plainly on record against the Germans and Pro-Germans who were filling America with their poisonous schemes. For we continued to entertain German diplomats and agents (paymasters, as they were, of murderers and plotters of arson) and to run on Germany's errands in various countries. The cry " He kept us out of war " was effectively used to reëlect Mr. Wilson, although members of the Government must have been thoroughly well aware that war was coming and coming soon.

It had long been Mr. Roosevelt's hope that if war came he might be allowed to raise a division, as he had once helped to raise a regiment, and take them, after suitable training, to the front. He knew where he could put his hands on the men, regular army officers, ex-volunteers and Rough Riders of the Spanish War, and other men of experience, who in turn could find other men, who could be made into soldiers, for they knew the important parts of a soldier's work, and could be trained quickly.

But the War Department and the President would have none of Mr. Roosevelt's services. The President replied that the high officers of the Army advised him against it, which was undoubtedly true. It is also extremely likely that the high officers of the Democratic Party would advise against letting Mr. Roosevelt serve his country, as they still feared him, and still vainly hoped that they could lessen his influence with the American people. Unlike President Lincoln, who would gladly accept the services of any man who could serve the country, Mr. Wilson could work only with men who were personally pleasing, who thought as he did on all subjects. The officer of the Army best known to European soldiers, and the one who trained one of the best divisions, was Roosevelt's old commander, General Leonard Wood. But he, like a statesman, had been advising preparedness for years, and he was therefore displeasing to the politicians who only began to prepare after war was declared. America and the Allies did not have the benefit of this distinguished officer's services in France.

Against the slothfulness of the Government in these years, Roosevelt voiced the true opinion of America. He did not merely criticize, for he offered his own services, and when he disapproved of what was being done, he pointed out what might be done by way of improvement. In spite of much condemnation of his course, his suggestions were nearly all adopted — six months or a year later. His offer to raise a division showed how many men were eager to fight, and spurred the Government into action.

The Germans and their friends in this country,

the peace-at-any-price folk who defended or apologized for the worst crimes of the Germans, and all the band of disloyal persons who think that patriotism is something to be sneered at,— all these hated Roosevelt with a deadly hatred. It was not a proud distinction to be numbered with these, and all who joined with them have made haste to forget the fact.

In his own family, his eldest son, Theodore Roosevelt, Jr., became first a Major and later a Lieutenant-Colonel of Infantry; Kermit and Archibald were both Captains; and Quentin was a Lieutenant in the Aviation force. His son-in-law, Dr. Richard Derby, was a Major in the Medical Corps. All of them sought active service, made every effort to get to the front, and succeeded. Two of them were wounded, and Quentin was killed in a battle in the air.

The death of his youngest son was a terrible blow to him, but he would not wince. His son had been true to his teaching; he had dared the high fortune of battle.

" You cannot bring up boys to be eagles," said he, " and expect them to act like sparrows! "

Some distinguished Japanese visitors calling on Mr. Roosevelt at this time came away deeply affected. To them he recalled the Samurai, with their noble traditions of utter self-sacrifice.

Throughout his life, but now as never before, he told his countrymen, there was no place in America for a divided loyalty. No German-Americans, nor Irish-Americans, nor Scotch-Americans. He would have no man try to split even, and be a " 50-50 American."

Shortly after war had ended, he sent this message to a patriotic meeting:

There must be no sagging back in the fight for Americanism merely because the war is over. Any man who says he is an American, but something else also, isn't an American at all. We have room for but one flag, the American flag, and this excludes the red flag, which symbolizes all wars against liberty and civilization, just as much as it excludes any foreign flag of a nation to which we are hostile. We have room for but one language here, and that is the English language, for we intended to see that the crucible turns our people out as Americans, of American nationality, and not as dwellers in a polyglot boarding-house; and we have room for but one soul loyalty, and that is loyalty to the American people.[1]

It was practically his last word to the country he had loved and served so well. That was on January 5, 1919.

Years before, when he and his children had played together, he had told them a story about lions. Some of the boys had been called the lion

[1] Hagedorn, p. 384.

cubs, and henceforth their father was to them
" The Old Lion."

On the sixth of January, one of his sons, who
was at home recovering from his wounds, sent a
message to his brothers in France :

The Old Lion is dead.

He was buried in a small cemetery near his
Long Island home.   A plain grave-stone marks
the place.   To his grave have come a King and a
Prince and other men of great name from Europe,
to lay wreaths there, as they put them on the
tombs of Washington and Lincoln.   But what
would have pleased him even more is that every
Sunday and holiday thousands of men, women
and children who knew him, thousands who loved
him, although they never saw him, men who
fought at his side, and men who fought against
him, go out to stand for a moment at his grave,
because they know him now as a wise, brave, and
patriotic American.

THE END

PRINTED IN THE UNITED STATES OF AMERICA